STUDENTS GUIDE TO THE DOCTRINE AND COVENANTS

By F. Henry Edwards

This guide consists of fifty-two lesson outlines and helps for a year of lesson studies of the revelations contained in sections 1 through 152 of the Doctrine and Covenants. The lessons are planned as a guide to students and teachers to accompany the use of the 1977 text, *A New Commentary on the Doctrine and Covenants*, by the same author.

Christian Education Office
Reorganized Church of Jesus Christ of
Latter Day Saints

ISBN 0-8309-0267-8

Printed in the United States of America

87 86 85 84   7 6 5 4

TABLE OF CONTENTS

INTRODUCING THE DOCTRINE AND COVENANTS

THE PERIOD OF 1861 - 1976

FOREWORD

There can be no doubt about the worth of the literary contribution of F. Henry Edwards to the life and faith of the Saints. For many years he was one of a very small group of leading ministers who wrote consistently to create a body of literature expressing the faith and hope of the church. His long years of service in the Council of Twelve and the First Presidency came at a time when it was possible for him to know and have fellowship with a great many of the members of the church. His name has been a household word. Many of the present leaders and members of the church grew up on his books. For this service and contribution there can never be a fully adequate statement of appreciation.

Since Brother Edwards has written over a long span of years, he has been among the first to recognize that the theological task is indeed a dynamic process. On occasion, when persons have asked him about his earlier writings he has often indicated that he could not write some of the same things in exactly the same way as they originally appeared. In the life of each person who really allows himself to grow under the Spirit of God there is a continuing need to understand that "instruction which has been given in former years is applicable in principle to the needs of today and should be so regarded by those who are seeking ways to accomplish the will of their heavenly Father. But the demands of a growing church require that these principles shall be evaluated and subjected to further interpretation" (D. and C. 147:7).

Brother Edwards has always had a dynamic faith

and has been consistently at the growing edge of the church. It is in the spirit of this quest that he has once more brought the value of his insights to the Saints in a *Students Guide to the Doctrine and Covenants.*

We are glad to commend this resource to the church in the spirit that Brother Edwards has expressed. "Pay attention to what you find interesting, and profitable. Have a good time." The process of the enrichment of our faith can be a joyful and fulfilling experience.

THE FIRST PRESIDENCY

Wallace B. Smith

Duane E. Couey

Howard S. Sheehy, Jr.

INTRODUCTION

A single-volume commentary on any of the standard books of the church must fall far short of completeness. It is the nature of scripture to invite studious explorations. Commenting on the results of such study takes time and space, so the commentary has to be selective. This means that there are unavoidable omissions.

In preparing my *New Commentary on the Book of Doctrine and Covenants* I felt reasonably safe in assuming that readers would use it to find relevant historical information not readily available to them, to call to mind other scriptures having a bearing on the revelations, and to find new cause to rejoice in the wonder of the loving wisdom of God. It was intended as a book for reference rather than as a text for individual or group study, but since the Christian Education Office has felt that a Study Guide might make the book usable also for consecutive study, this is my endeavor to help to that end.

In preparing the guide I have tried to keep the following in mind: Our concern in studying the Doctrine and Covenants is that we may understand the will of God more truly in order to obey it more fully and more gratefully.

The inspired documents (hereafter referred to as revelations) in the Doctrine and Covenants were given to meet specific situations, but they also embody and illustrate principles of permanent value. The sections headed "For Consideration" are intended to call attention to these principles and areas of modern life where they should be applied.

Like other scriptures, the Doctrine and Covenants should be studied in the mood of worship. We shall have little profit if we come to our study in search of proof texts with which to bolster opinions already held. Our opinions need constant adjustment upward so as to conform more soundly to a wisdom far greater than our own.

Here are some observations in connection with the use of the guide:

- The study is divided into five lessons to introduce the Doctrine and Covenants; thirty-five lessons on the revelations through Joseph Smith, Jr.; and twelve lessons covering the period 1861-1976. This division is made for purposes of convenience only. Students should feel free, of course, to rearrange these lessons, combining or omitting any of them.

- Few of the revelations deal with a single topic only. This has required me to jump around a little, but I have sought to maintain the chronological sequences of the Doctrine and Covenants and the *New Commentary* as fully as possible. Students whose primary interest is in topical studies will find it necessary to jump around a little more. The lesson headings may give some minor help.

- Some questions will arise naturally in the course of class study or while reading the *New Commentary*, e.g., questions whose purpose is to impress specific quotations or procedures. I have omitted such questions since serious students will frame their own better than anyone else can do for them, and also because it has been necessary to conserve space. One result has been that by using the saved space I have been able to make the guide a minor supplement to the *New Commentary*.

- Study the Doctrine and Covenants, using the *New Commentary* and the *Students Guide* as aids to understanding, but never as substitutes for what you believe is the clear intent of the scriptural text.

I have had to include more comments and questions than any one student is likely to find time to study. Pay attention to what you find interesting and profitable.

Have a good time.

F. Henry Edwards

Exploration 1
DIVINE REVELATION

PREPARATORY READING: *New Commentary,* pages 7-18

Introduction

This chapter is essentially preparatory to the lessons of the entire course. It centers in the nature of divine revelation and its vital importance in the Christian life. Students of the revelations should look for the disclosure of the nature of God which lies behind the specific references in revelatory documents. These are not to be understood by mere intellectual inquiry. Understanding draws on the total resources of disciples and, particularly, on their Godlikeness.

Revelation involves three basic elements: a loving Father, needy children, and capacity on the part of these children to understand that which the Father wishes to communicate. Behind every revelation are love and holiness. These may well be used as tests of the divinity of that which claims our attention.

For Consideration

Our heavenly Father has laid the foundation for his self-disclosure in that (a) people are created with built-in capacities for response to him; (b) he has sent his Son to reveal the true nature of God in the lives of humans (*New Commentary,* pages 9, 10); (c) he leads those who heed the way of understanding through the ministry of the Holy Spirit.

Our highest thought of God—illuminating, challenging, and sustaining—is that he wants us to know and love him and to rejoice in him. This is possible only as he makes himself known to us. People by their searching cannot find him.

Revelation is an inner experience. There is no divine revelation without inspired discernment. This is more than the acknowledgment of facts; it is a conviction of truth spoken in love (*New Commentary*, pages 10,15).

Revelation is never complete; we are finite and revelation is limted to our capacity. Greater understanding of divinity and of the purpose of God awaits our growth. Meanwhile, our heavenly Father communicates himself to us as fully as we allow (*New Commentary*, pages 11-13).

The revelations in the Book of Doctrine and Covenants were received by people and the church in specific situations as a means of increasing their understanding, guiding their actions, and deepening their devotion. If we are to understand these revelations, they must be studied in relation to the circumstances under which they were received. They were not isolated pronouncements but part of the warp and woof of our church history.

When properly understood and incorporated into the life of the church, earlier instructions, including earlier scriptures, become the basis of further instruction. Principles revealed in earlier days are thus elaborated as the experience of the individual and the church becomes more mature.

The revelation of God is still growing in the lives of people and in the life of the church. This revelation is in experience rather than in a written record, although the written record preserves our memory of the original experience and is a means of further inspiration under the illumination of the Spirit of God. It is not possible to scale the heights of spiritual understanding at one bound, but with eternity before us, and the assurance of the unfailing love of God, those who put their trust in God can grow from grace to grace.

Questions and Discussion Topics

1. Discuss revelation as a function of the Holy Spirit.
2. What is the relation between revelation and discovery? What part does God play in divine revelation? What part do humans play?
3. Discuss the relation between character and insight. Can a person who is at enmity with God fully understand the divine purpose? Give reasons.
4. In what sense is religion a solitary adventure? In what sense is it a social experience? In what sense is it a historical experience?
5. In what sense has the process of revelation come to its culmination in the life of Jesus Christ? In what sense is it still going forward? Explain your answers.
6. Why is revelation adapted to our world? Discuss, briefly, the necessity for acquaintance with the background of the revelations in Doctrine and Covenants in order to rightly understand them.
7. Explain the difference between the "revelatory experience" and the "record of the revelatory experience" (see pages 16-18 in the *New Commentary*).

Exploration 2

REVELATION AND ITS RECORD

PREPARATORY READING: *New Commentary*, **pages 14-26, 256-258**

ADDITIONAL BOOKS NEEDED: Doctrine and Covenants, Bible

Introduction

The Doctrine and Covenants contains the record of revelatory experiences through the prophets of our dispensation. This record is of major importance to the church, but its function must be understood by the light of the Holy Spirit and against the background of our history. Its own revelation of its value is a progressive experience.

For Consideration

The communication of new information may be denoted a "revelation." At first glance this may seem to be all that is involved—for example, in the announcement of calls to new responsibilities such as constitute part of many of the sections of the Doctrine and Covenants. But in *divine* revelation more than this is involved. For those who have eyes to see and hearts to understand, divine revelation reaches beyond what words can convey (D. and C. 125:conclusion; 131:1b, c).

Consider the beauties of nature or the soul-searching qualities of great music, painting, or poetry. What is achieved here beyond that which words can

15

express? What message, if any, does this have for you concerning the nature of divine revelation?

The phrasing of the revelations is important, but grammar and style are not of primary importance. In this connection note the disquietude of some of the early elders over the language used by Joseph Smith, Jr., and how this was dispersed (D. and C. 67:2; *New Commentary*, pages 256-258).

Consider some of the values to be found in public reading of the scriptures. Have someone read the Sacrament prayers so as to clarify and impress their meaning. Note that different emphases may be called for in different circumstances, yet remain consistent with each other.

Joseph Smith III wrote more than his father or any of his sons concerning the experience of revelation. In certain of his presentations he said, "being commanded of the Spirit I arose from my praying and wrote. . ." (D. and C. 122:Introduction); "I was in the Spirit and was commanded to write. . ." (D. and C. 124:Introduction); "I was in the Spirit, the Spirit of inspiration burning in my breast; and by it I was bidden to come to the house of assembly and *tell* what was given to me of light and instruction" (D. and C. 125:Introduction). Note the evident importance of the word of revelation, but note also the authority gained through such testimony as the foregoing (see also D. and C. 139:2; 147:Introduction).

All ministers of the church are called to teach and expound the scriptures (D. and C. 17:8d, 10a, 11f). The patriarch-evangelist appears to have special responsibility here (D. and C. 125:5). Consider the purpose and importance of such teaching and expounding of the written word in terms of the broadening and understanding of the meaning intended.

In some of the revelations the instruction given confirms and/or applies to that given in earlier scriptures. Apparently the intent is that which is renewed shall be heeded at a deeper level. Consider revelations in the Doctrine and Covenants from this point of view, e.g., Sections 4; 10:6-7; 12:4a; 117:5; 122:17.

Comment on the availability of the scriptures as a ground of unity among the disciples. What more is required? What is the essential foundation of spiritual unity?

Questions and Discussion Topics
1. Is the only revelation of the nature and purpose of divinity to be found in the standard books of the church? If not, where else may such revelation be found?
2. The supreme and final revelation of the nature of divinity is in the life and teachings of Jesus Christ. Why could no adequate revelation be complete other than that through Jesus Christ?
3. Apparently Jesus left no written record of his teachings. Why do you think this was so? If he had done so, would it have conveyed his teaching fully? Why or why not? Do our present scriptures fully convey this teaching? If not, what more is needed?
4. Paul wrote that "Our gospel came not unto you in word only, but also in power, and in the Holy

17

Ghost, and in much assurance" (I Thessalonians 1:5). Discuss this in the light of importance to the scriptures in the Christian enterprise.

5. What is "expounding" (D. and C. 17:10a, 11f; 24:2c)? What bearing on such expounding has the instruction to "seek ye out of the best books words of wisdom; seek learning even by study, and also by faith" (D. and C. 85:36a)?

6. How are the deeper meanings of the revelations likely to become more apparent to students of the scriptures than to casual readers? Why?

7. Note the value of revelation which confirms what can be found in earlier revelations. Discuss the added value of reading the scriptures as though they were addressed to you personally.

8. Summarize your understanding of the importance of the record of Doctrine and Covenants revelations in the life of the church and in your life. How may these values be augmented?

Exploration 3

CONDITIONS OF DIVINE REVELATION

PREPARATORY READING: *New Commentary*, **pages 13-14, 188-190, 236, 312-313, 403, 419, 422, 454, 501-502, 545; Church History, Volume 1, pages 8-10, 45-47**

ADDITIONAL BOOKS NEEDED: Bible, Book of Mormon, Doctrine and Covenants

Introduction

Divine self-disclosure is according to the grace of God. We can neither demand it nor earn it (D. and C. 22:1; 36:1c). The revelatory experiences recorded in the Doctrine and Covenants have been given according to the will of God but, in a secondary sense, according to the attitude of the recipients. Some revelatory documents recorded long ago become meaningful in our life as a disciple—revelations in truth—as the Spirit of God quickens our spiritual perception.

For Consideration

The basic need of all human beings has led to revelations through the prophets; in the life, ministry, death, resurrection, and appearances of Jesus Christ; in the all-pervading ministry of the Holy Spirit; in the apostolic witness; in the preparation and preservation of the scriptures; and in the Restoration.

We must abide by the conditions of divine revelation if we are to learn the riches of the kingdom of heaven. Such revelation is both a prelude to spiritual growth and the goal of that growth. It is both the means and the end.

Revelation depends on faith in God (Hebrews 11:6). Faith is more than acceptance of certain affirmations about God. It includes awareness of our own limitation and openness to divine guidance. Faith may be very small and tentative (Alma 16:152-158), but it cannot be neutral.

Faith in God is evidenced in prayer and, often, in fasting. It has notes of inquiry and of pre-commitment. Such faith was a condition of the revelations in the Doctrine and Covenants: faith on the part of the seeker and on the part of those blessed by the light received (James 1:5-7; D. and C. 16:4c; 42:18d; 59:1).

We are so constituted that we can receive divine revelation only when we are spiritually alert. It may well be that a major task of the Holy Spirit is to quicken this alertness (D. and C. 42:17).

Prayers for guidance in known areas of need are approved of God. Frequently revelation has been received in response to a need expressed by the body: the Preface (D. and C. 1), the duties of the Twelve (D. and C. 104, 120, 122), changes in the Bishopric (D. and C. 135), and the call of patriarchs (D. and C. 126:7, 13; 137:4b; 145:6a-c).

An attitude of obedience toward revelation already received prepares the way for further revelation as it may be necessary. But mere intellectual alertness is not sufficient. Just as we need to share the lives of others in order to understand their motives and their purposes, so also we need to share the life of God in order to gain a more adequate conception of goodwill toward us.

There is sound reason for supporting the Prophet in our prayers. This focuses the attention of the group, ministering to our faith and unity, and is a source of strength to the one chosen of God to minister to us. This does not decry insights quickened in other ways, but it does impose important and necessary disciplines on the Prophet, on the quorums, on individual ministers, and the Saints in general (D. and C. 43:1-2, 3d; 104:11b; 125:14; see also *New Commentary*, pages 188-190; 454).

Questions and Discussion Topics

1. Comment on these religious factors in divine revelation: the nature of our heavenly Father, the nature of our creation, and the receptivity of human beings.
2. Faith is a gift of God. What is the relation of faith to a person's life of prayer and service? How is faith involved in the further disclosure of the will of God?
3. Discuss the relation of the sense of need to the receipt of divine revelation. Do such needs as are felt and expressed always lead to the receipt of the guidance required? Explain. How is the time element important here (John 16:12)?
4. Comment on how such qualities as sympathy and kindliness help us to understand others. In what ways does actual sharing in the work of God help us to understand the nature and purpose of God? With these questions as background discuss the

relation between saintly living and divine revelation.

5. Discuss the relation of openness to newly perceived truths to the humility which is a prerequisite of revelation.

6. In what mood (spirit) must we study the scriptures in order for them to become a means of divine enlightment? Share evidences that "the Lord has yet more light and truth to break forth from his word."

7. What is a basic reason underlying the repeated admonition in modern revelation to "sustain each other in peace" (D. and C. 117:13; 140:1b)?

8. It has been said that one of the major functions of the Prophet is to lead disciples to become a prophetic people. What burdens which rest on the Prophet because of his office must be shared by others if this ideal is to be reached?

Exploration 4

PUBLISHING THE REVELATIONS

PREPARATORY READING: *New Commentary,* **pages 27-32, 68-71, 73-75, 94-95**

ADDITIONAL BOOKS NEEDED: Doctrine and Covenants

Introduction

The Book of Commandments was produced under great difficulties. The work of the compilers and printers was appreciated by their colleagues who knew of these difficulties. The shortcomings of the Book of Commandments were readily admitted by those most intimately concerned in the publication of the documents in Kirtland in 1835 and in the compilation of the contents of the Doctrine and Covenants which appeared in August of that year.

For Consideration

Many of the early revelations were addressed to individuals and it is not likely that these were widely circulated. It was of great importance, however, that those revelations dealing with the basic beliefs and structure of the church be available to the leaders whose message and responsibilities needed to be clearly understood. Fortunately, most of these leaders were available as the major centers developed: first, Joseph Smith, Jr., Oliver Cowdery, and Frederick G. Williams and shortly thereafter, Parley P. Pratt, Sidney Rigdon, Edward Partridge, and W. W. Phelps.

Many of the early conferences of the church were essentially administrative councils called by Joseph Smith, Jr., as needs arose and as group understanding and agreement were desired. Such a conference authorized the purchase of a press and type which was set up in Independence. Publication of the revelations in *The Evening and the Morning Star* was important, but a more permanent record was needed. The issue of the Book of Commandments was a logical and necessary step forward.

The title page of the Book of Commandments shows that its major concern was "the government of the Church of Christ" (*New Commentary*, page 31). Except for typographical errors the revelations were identical with those appearing in the *Star*.

Printing was proceeding on July 20, 1833, when a mob destroyed the printing office, pied the type, and scattered the printed pages. The Book of Commandments was never completed, but some of the printed sheets were gathered for individual use. Some may have been sent to Kirtland prior to the mob action. Several compilations of the sheets have been published from time to time.

The revelations published in the *Star* and the Book of Commandments were from copies. The originals remained with Joseph Smith in Kirtland. The *Star* resumed publication there and in September 1834 its first and second volumes were reissued. Note was taken of the "many errors, typographical and others" and a promise was made that the new compilation would be compared with the original which was now available. It was also noted that other items from the revelations had been added (*New Commentary*, pages 31-32).

The Book of Commandments was too incomplete to fulfill the purpose prompting its preparation. It was never accepted by the church. Those most directly concerned with its compilation regarded the 1835 edition of the Doctrine and Covenants as filling the general purpose of the book more fully than did the unfinished Book of Commandments itself.

There were a few interpolations in the revelations as they appeared in the 1835 edition of the Doctrine and Covenants in contrast with the version in the Book of Commandments. Possibly the most notable from the viewpoint of church organization is in Doctrine and Covenants 17:16-17. The inclusion of these paragraphs was fully consistent with the manner of compilation of this revelation (*New Commentary*, pages 94-95). They represent guidance received to meet the growth of the membership which was a specialization of functions within the eldership (*New Commentary*, page 105).

The statement concerning the gift of Aaron in Doctrine and Covenants 8:3 is different than that in the Book of Commandments (*New Commentary*, pages 73-75). There seems to be no evidence that this disturbed Oliver Cowdery, who was most directly concerned, or any of the early elders. There may be an explanation which has escaped commentators. Changes here and in the revelation concerning continuance of John the Beloved (D. and C. 7, *New Commentary*, pages 68-71) throw light on the nature of revelation and its phrasing in changing circumstances.

There are no significant differences between the doctrinal and leadership teachings of the Book of Commandments and the Doctrine and Covenants. Yet the Book of Commandments is important in relation to church history and to the process of revelation.

Questions and Discussion Topics

1. How were the copies of the early revelations preserved? How widely were they circulated? How did early leaders know the content of those revelations which were especially important to the growing church?

2. What was the name of the first paper published by the church? When was it published? Where? Who was its editor? What contents were particularly important at the time and in light of later history?

3. The revelation now Doctrine and Covenants 70:1 called six of the elders "to be stewards over the revelations and commandments." Who were they? What was their most immediate task? Suggest why each was included. The committee which compiled the 1835 edition of the Doctrine and Covenants included four of these. Why were these included? Why were the others no longer retained?

4. What was the purpose of the Book of Commandments? Was it intended to include the "appendix"? (See Introduction to Doctrine and Covenants 108.) Summarize the evidence that it was replaced by the Doctrine and Covenants.

5. What is meant by "plenary inspiration"? (See *Restoration Scriptures* by Richard P. Howard, pages 12-13.) Which revelations appear to have

been phrased by the Prophet to convey light received by him (D. and C. 101:11d; 121:1b, 2b; 125: introduction)? How may the wording by a prophet indicate plenary revelation, when in reality it is his best understanding of God's revealment?

6. With the growth of the church, functions at first shared among the elders were restricted to the quorums and councils. At times this was indicated by the inclusion of the revelation directing such organization and at times by the insertion of additional paragraphs at relevant points in earlier revelations (D. and C. 17:16, 17). Does this procedure seem to you to be reasonable? Explain.

7. There have been a number of reprintings of the Book of Commandments. This book has value to historians and to those interested in church doctrine. It has been reprinted by Herald House. What value, if any, does it have other than that covered in a general fashion for this lesson?

Exploration 5

EDITIONS OF THE DOCTRINE AND COVENANTS

PREPARATORY READING: *New Commentary*, pages 32-44; Church History, Volume 1, Chapters 10, 19, 22; *Journal of History*, Volume 14, page 139

ADDITIONAL BOOKS NEEDED: *Restoration Scriptures* by Richard P. Howard

Introduction

The Doctrine and Covenants is one of the three standard books of the church. Our concern here is with how it came into being, its purpose, and its authority.

For Consideration

Publication of the Doctrine and Covenants was authorized by members of the Standing High Council who appointed a committee consisting of the First Presidency, plus Oliver Cowdery, who were described as "Presiding Elders" of the church. Oliver had been intimately connected with the copying and early publication of the revelations.

The early numbers of the *Star* were reissued at Kirtland in 1835 while steps were being taken to present the revelations in more permanent form as had been intended in the Book of Commandments. This was important since the *Star* contained corrected versions of the revelations which had been published in Independence, and these earlier printings were available to those who would approve the Doctrine and Covenants.

The "Lectures on Faith" and the articles on Marriage, Government, and Laws in General were not revelations. The Lectures have been omitted since the edition of 1897. The other two articles are retained as part of the text of the 1970 edition (D. and C. 111, 112) and were not transferred to the appendix.

The 1844 Doctrine and Covenants was published after the death of Joseph Smith, Jr. Note the additions (*New Commentary*, page 37). The Mormon Doctrine and Covenants was used in the Reorganization until the Cincinnati edition of 1864 was printed. In general it followed the 1844 format but added Sections 22 and 36.

The action of the semiannual General Conference of 1878 relating to the Doctrine and Covenants does not mention the Lectures on Faith or the articles on Marriage and Government. Only the revelations are included as part of the "standard of authority" (*New Commentary*, pages 39-40). But the New Revised Edition of the Doctrine and Covenants published in 1897 did include the minutes of the 1894 Joint Council. These minutes now appear, more consistently, as Appendix E.

The expression "the Standard Books of the Church" needs to be explored. The Doctrine and Covenants can hardly be fully standard when there is no consensus on some of the revelations. The same is true of the other scriptures, including the Book of Mormon. Perhaps the term points the way to a needed unity of understanding.

The types of revelations in the Doctrine and Covenants have changed. The nearest approach to the personal revelations of earlier times (D. and C. 4-6, 8-10) appears to be in the revelation through President W. Wallace Smith (D. and C. 150:1; 151:5a). The timing of such revelations as constitute the Doctrine and Covenants has also changed (D. and C. 140:4b; 149:1; 151:5b).

Both the number and the quality of the early revelations were directly influenced by the eager expectancies of the Saints and by the importance of their pioneering in kingdom building. Recovery of this expectancy and renewed activity in the specific work of the kingdom would create both the need and the atmosphere for further divine guidance.

Questions and Discussion Topics

1. Cite the steps taken toward the publication of the 1835 edition of the Doctrine and Covenants. By whom was this edition compiled? How did it become one of the Standard Books of the Church?
2. What were the contents of the 1835 Doctrine and Covenants? How well informed of the contents of this edition were the members of the church who approved it?
3. How do the format and contents of the Doctrine and Covenants differ from that of the Book of Commandments? Which revelations appeared first in the Doctrine and Covenants? Why?
4. What were the Lectures on Faith? Why are they no longer a part of the Doctrine and Covenants? Where are they found?

5. When was the second edition of the Doctrine and Covenants published? By whose authority? What had been added? Which of the new sections have been retained as part of the body of the 1970 edition?
6. Name some important editions of the Doctrine and Covenants issued by the Reorganization. What new sections were added? By what authority? How fully is the Restoration committed to the statements concerning Joseph Smith, Jr., in Doctrine and Covenants 113 (Appendix D)?
7. Why do so many revelations to individuals appear in the early sections of the Doctrine and Covenants? Are similar revelations available today? Why? Why does the Doctrine and Covenants contain so many more revelations through Joseph Smith, Jr., than through his successors in office?
8. What is the Doctrine and Covenants? What is its place in the church of today?

THE PERIOD OF JOSEPH SMITH, JR.

Exploration 6

THE PREFACE

PREPARATORY READING: *New Commentary*, **pages 44-48; Church History, Volume 1, pages 221-222.**

ADDITIONAL BOOKS NEEDED: Doctrine and Covenants

Introduction

This revelation, given when the church was about nineteen months old, was intended as an introduction to the Book of Commandments. It should be noted that more than sixty of the revelations which came after the Preface in the Doctrine and Covenants were given before it in time. This Preface should be studied both in its historical setting and for the permanent values embodied in it.

For Consideration

The Preface sets forth the attitudes and points of view already accepted in the church. It carries strong notes of certainty: authority, warning, universal purpose, and the awfulness of apostasy (D. and C. 1:5a-c). We should capture these dominant notes at the beginning of our course of study. They were characteristic of the early Restoration.

The Preface and the revelations it introduces are addressed to the people of the church and also to people from "afar" (D. and C. 1:1, 3). Persons who are not members of the church are not likely to be aware of this. Evidently missionary testimony is envisioned. But it should be noted, also, that this testimony should be consistent with the message of the Doctrine and Covenants. Disciples, realizing this, should study the revelations so as to be familiar with their teachings, obligations, and promises (D. and C. 1:7, 8).

The note of warning sounded in the Preface and repeated many times in other revelations was more in tune with the times in 1830 than it is today. But it is still sound, the evidence justifying it having multiplied down the years. To warn "the unbelieving and rebellious" (D. and C. 1:2c) as did the Lord Jesus and to do so in his spirit is not to threaten but to seek to save.

The revelations in the Doctrine and Covenants derive their authority from their truth as attested by the Spirit of God and as vindicated in the experience of disciples. They may have secondary authority, but the validation of the Spirit is primary.

Apostasy is generally the result of "straying" from the divine ordinances (D. and C. 1:3d). It is rarely the result of a considered judgment. It is often due to failure to "meet together often" (D. and C. 17:11b). Strategy in overcoming it may well center here, before the "straying" begins.

Give thought to the horror felt by those dedicated

to the helping professions over conditions which
defeat the need of men, women, and children for
health, education, employment, dignity. We cannot all
be social workers, but neither can we stand aloof
from ungodly social situations in view of the nature of
this Preface.

Many thoughtful people believe that the basic sin of
our age, as of every age, is idolatry: "Every man
walketh in his own way, and after the image of his
own god, whose image is in the likeness of the world,
and whose substance is that of an idol" (D. and C.
1:3e). Consider this in relation to our secular age.
Records of revelatory experiences in the Doctrine and
Covenants contain notes of universal moral and
spiritual appeal. Be alert to recognize them, respond
to them, and share them.

Questions and Discussion Topics

1. State the circumstances under which the revelation
   known as "The Preface" was received. Where
   would it appear if it took its chronological position
   in the Doctrine and Covenants? What diverse
   purposes should it serve?
2. List and comment on the purposes of the
   Restoration indicated in the Preface.
3. What is the purpose of the note of warning
   sounded in the Doctrine and Covenants? Is this
   note found here only or is it characteristic of
   Christian scripture and preaching?
4. Do you find palatable the message of warning?
   Why? What precautions does this suggest for those
   who are commissioned to "warn, expound, exhort,

and teach, and invite all to come unto Christ"
(D. and C. 17:11f) and to preach "with the warning
voice . . . until the world is warned" (D. and C.
122:8c)?

5. What do we mean when we talk of apostasy? In its
   essence is it apostasy from an organization, from a
   doctrine, or from God? Explain.
6. Many who were once members of the church no
   longer walk with us. Enumerate typical
   inducements to apostasy, e.g., failure to receive
   ministry in terms of needs; failure to use talents
   worthily; engrossment in scholastic, business,
   recreational, cultic, or other personal interests.
   Suggest steps we should take to assist the Saints as
   they face and wrestle with the temptation of
   apathy, withdrawal, zealousness? How can we
   establish these as safeguards instead of merely
   discussing them?
7. Consider the relation of genuine worship and
   lasting (as against short-term remedial) social
   ministries. Do you agree with Archbishop Temple
   that the most urgent need of people is the
   experience of worship? Why? What does the
   experience of worship do for us? Some have felt
   that worship leads to service. How does this
   provide insight into relationships between worship
   and social ministries?
8. If a talented writer, endowed with spiritual insight,
   gave you his or her paraphrase of the Preface what
   would be your reaction? What would happen if
   you shared it in the spirit of worship with a small
   group of earnest disciples?

Exploration 7

REVELATIONS CONCERNING THE BOOK OF MORMON

PREPARATORY READING: *New Commentary,* **pages 48-56, 59-62, 87-90, 301;** *Restoration Scriptures* **by Richard Howard, Chapter 2**

ADDITIONAL BOOKS NEEDED: Church History, Volume 1; Doctrine and Covenants; Bible

Introduction

The first task of Joseph Smith in connection with the Restoration was the translation and publication of the Book of Mormon. Several of the early revelations naturally have to do with this important work.

For Consideration

The translation of the Book of Mormon was not automatic. Joseph's gifts and limitations were important factors (D. and C. 3:1d; 9:3). If there are faults they are human mistakes. This was so even if the key factor was "the mercy. . . [and]. . . power of God" (D. and C. 1:3, 5d). The process of translation was therefore an important educational experience. This is attested by the testimony of Joseph concerning the approach to the restoration of the Aaronic priesthood (Church History, Volume 1, page 3).

Although Joseph was the key figure in the translation of the Book of Mormon, the work was made possible by the contribution of many others who supplied basic needs. Note the roles of the Smith family, and of Oliver Cowdery, Martin Harris, the Whitmers, and the Knights.

It is almost impossible to overrate the importance of witnesses in the Christian enterprise. The testimony of the resurrection was committed to "witnesses chosen before of God" (Acts 10:39-45). The corroborative testimony of Oliver Cowdery concerning the restoration of the Aaronic priesthood is of major historical and spiritual importance (Church History, Volume 1, pages 37-39).

The qualifications required of the Book of Mormon witnesses pertained to their basic character—humility, faith, sincerity (D. and C. 5:5b; 15:1c). Their testimonies bear marks of their verisimilitude, e.g. the eight witnesses saw and "hefted"—felt the weight of—the plates. Every one of them maintained his testimony throughout his life. No profit of any kind accrued to any of them except the satisfaction of maintaining his testimony.

Many of the early Saints were converted through the Book of Mormon. It was probably the major missionary tool of the elders. The early Saints were commanded to teach the principles found there (D. and C. 42:5a). The failure of some to do so brought them under condemnation (D. and C. 83:8a-b).

The Book of Mormon affirmed the unchanging purpose of God through successive dispensations (D. and C. 2:6, 3:15). This was a basic factor in the restoration of the priesthood. It gave the Saints an expansive sense of the underlying unity of humanity, kinship with the spiritual giants of past ages, and understanding of the unchanging importance of obedience to the principles of the gospel.

It is unfortunate that so much effort had been put forth to vindicate the claims of believers as to the manner of the coming forth of the Book of Mormon in contrast to endeavors to explore, explain, and apply its teachings. The teachings of the Book of Mormon bear scrutiny.

Questions and Discussion Topics

1. What was Joseph Smith's part in the coming forth of the Book of Mormon? Did his personal character support his claims? Comment on the support given him in this connection by all the members of his immediate family: his parents; Hyrum, his older brother; William; Samuel H.; Don Carlos; his sisters Catherine and Sophronia; his wife Emma.

2. Note that part of the Book of Mormon translation was lost. What was the responsibility of Joseph and the principles laid down in this connection (D. and C. 2:2b)?

3. Who were the three witnesses? Who were the eight witnesses? What do you consider their basic qualifications? Where may their testimonies be found? Do you consider their testimonies to be credible? If so, why? If not, why? Why were the Book of Mormon plates shown only to these persons?

4. Who were Joseph's chief assistants in the work of translation? When was the Book of Mormon published? What became of the original and printer's copy of the Book of Mormon? (Review

Chapter 2 in *Restoration Scriptures* by Richard P. Howard for information.)

5. What is the stated purpose of the Book of Mormon? What is its relation to the other standard books?

6. What plates are mentioned in connection with the Book of Mormon (*New Commentary*, pages 53, 87-90)? What other ancient artifacts are mentioned with the plates?

7. Comment on the value of the Book of Mormon as a missionary tool. How is it a Restoration distinctive?

8. Comment on the importance of Joseph's work as translator of the Book of Mormon and as reviser of the Bible in relation to his insight into the nature of revelation and the function of scripture.

Exploration 8

DISPENSATIONS OF THE GOSPEL

PREPARATORY READING: *New Commentary*, **pages 97-98, 68-71, 129-131, 157-162**

ADDITIONAL BOOKS NEEDED: Doctrine and Covenants, Bible, Book of Mormon

Introduction

The early Saints saw the purpose of divinity as encompassing all time and eternity, with succeeding "dispensations" related to each other. This is a major teaching of the Book of Mormon. With such a faith they regarded the Restoration as the culmination of the hopes and labors of men and women of other days—the "dispensation of the fullness of time."

For Consideration

The early Christians believed that Peter, James, and John saw Moses and Elias with Jesus on the Mount of Transfiguration (Matthew 17:1-3, II Peter 1:16-18). They knew that in the coming of the Lord Jesus something totally unprecedented had happened, but they believed that this had been anticipated down the ages (Acts 3:21-24, 10:42; Hebrews 1:1). Their faith is reflected in the New Testament (Galatians 3:8, 14; Hebrews 3:14-4:2).

After the close of the apostolic age the Christian church experienced times of "falling away" which the apostles had anticipated taking place (II Thessalonians 2:2-3; II Timothy 3:1-5, 4:3-4; Acts 20:28-30). This does not mean that nothing of the light of truth remained, for God's Spirit was present. The earlier fullness of the gospel was lost and many errors were taught as of God. Many good men and women sought to serve God and were blessed. However, at times the institutional church lost sight of its purpose.

The experiences of Joseph leading to the publication of the Book of Mormon and the restoration of the priesthood quickened in him the conviction that our heavenly Father has revealed himself to people in successive ages, thus laying the foundation for Joseph's own ministry.

The Saints of the early Restoration believed themselves to be living in a time of culmination, a time of refreshing, a time of the "restitution of all things spoken by the mouths of the holy prophets." This was a time when all things would be gathered together in one and the hopes of the righteous would be fulfilled in the triumphant preaching of the gospel to people of every nation.

With such an expansive concept of God and of his continuing work in the world, it was inevitable that the Saints should believe that the principles of the gospel are eternal in their nature. They could not think of these principles as the product of human beings groping after light, but as truth revealed from heaven for salvation.

The sections numbered as Doctrine and Covenants 22 and 36 were not included in the Doctrine and Covenants during the lifetime of Joseph Smith, although they were received in June and December, 1830. They occur in the editions of the Doctrine and

Covenants published by the Reorganization and are part of the Inspired Version of the Old Testament.

The expression "the fullness of the gospel" is used many times in the Doctrine and Covenants (D. and C. 26:2a). It challenges and rewards exploration. But, fundamentally, it refers to the event of God's love in history—Christ. From this meaning we see it as a way of life which cannot be described in words alone. Consider the fullness of the gospel as being understood only (a) under the guidance of the Holy Spirit, (b) by those who love and seek to serve God, and (c) within the fellowship of such disciples. Under these conditions it grows "brighter and brighter, until the perfect day" (D. and C. 50:6b).

Questions and Discussion Topics

1. Do you agree that the conditions of eternal life are unchanging from age to age? Why? Why not?
2. Discuss the assurance that grew in the apostle Peter following his experience at the Mount of Transfiguration (II Peter 1:16). Note the breadth of vision concerning the work of God derived from such an experience.
3. Imagine yourself deprived of the guidance given to men and women of earlier ages and enumerate some of the lacks which would ensue.
4. What was the relation of John the Baptist to the Restoration movement? Moroni? Peter, James, and John? Why are these important today?
5. What is the meaning of the term "dispensation"? What do we mean by the "dispensation of the fullness of time"? Suggest some biblical phrases

which have a related meaning.

6. Name some men and women used of God between the apostolic age and the beginning of the Restoration. For what spiritual treasures are we indebted to such persons?

7. Consider, briefly, the social nature of salvation: that people of good intent need the support of others of good intent in order to understand the purpose of God. How does this include cooperation with them in the achievement of this purpose?

8. Enumerate some of the statements regarding the nature and work of God which are contained in the sections under consideration. Note the continuing ministries of great spiritual workers beyond the point of their physical death.

Exploration 9

INSTRUCTION TO EARLY CONVERTS

PREPARATORY READING: *New Commentary,*
pages 57-59, 62-68, 77-87

ADDITIONAL BOOKS NEEDED: Doctrine and
Covenants, Bible

Introduction

A group of earnest and spiritually minded
persons soon surrounded Joseph. Each wanted
guidance in regard to his or her part in the
Restoration movement. The revelations given in
answer to their inquiries cover common ground
and show considerable duplication. Therefore, they
are considered together.

For Consideration

The prophecy of the coming forth of the
"marvelous work" of the restoration was given
more than a year prior to the organization of the
church and bears indirect evidence of the patience
with which Joseph awaited specific instruction to
organize. The expression came from Isaiah 29:14
which may be studied in this connection.

The statement that "if ye have desires to serve
God ye are called to the work" is contained in the
revelation addressed to Joseph Smith, Sr., in
February 1829.

Some of the essential conditions of effective service
are set forth in the early records: desires to serve

(D. and C. 4:1c, 6:2, 10:2, 11:2); faith, hope, charity, and love, with an eye single to the glory of God (D. and C. 4:1e, 6:8c); concern for wisdom prior to riches (D. and C. 6:3b); sobriety, temperance, patience (D. and C. 6:8c); trust in "that Spirit which leadeth to do good" (D. and C. 10:6); humility, love (D. and C. 11:4b). These are still fundamental. No material or intellectual offerings can be acceptable substitutes for them.

The command to "seek to bring forth and establish the cause of Zion" was sounded a year before the organization of the church. It was no afterthought. It was (and is) of importance to consider Zion as a *Cause*—an enterprise of ultimate worth. It has to be brought into our beings and established as a way of life.

Consider the command to "say nothing but repentance to this generation" (D. and C. 10:4b, 14:3) in terms of its inclusiveness and its unchanging timeliness.

Responsibilities attach to the gifts of God to people. Oliver was told, *"Exercise* thy gift" (D. and C. 6:5c). He and Joseph were told, *"Magnify* thy office" (D. and C. 23:2a). Oliver, Hyrum, David, and others were told, *"Give heed* unto my word" (D. and C. 6:1, 10:1, 11:1). But to Joseph Knight this was said with added emphasis: "Give heed *with your might"* (D. and C. 11:5b).

Some of the phrases of the early records have become characteristic of Restoration thought and expression: "The Cause of Zion," "a marvelous work and a wonder," "Seek not for riches, but for wisdom," or "Say nothing but repentance to this generation." The nature of the Restoration *movement* must be considered in light of such expressions.

Questions and Discussion Topics

1. Name the conditions of effective service set forth in these revelations. What does each mean? What does their announcement indicate about Joseph Smith? What priority do they have over other conditions of service?
2. Who are called to serve God? How do you know?
3. Give a working definition of repentance in light of the command to "say nothing but repentance to this generation." Why is repentance given such prominence? Differentiate between repentance and repenting.
4. What is meant by the "Cause of Zion"? Why was this process mentioned so early in the revelations?
5. Enumerate some of the promises recorded in the early sections of the Doctrine and Covenants. What conditions are attached? What are similar promises and conditions today?
6. Hyrum Smith was told that he was "called" (D. and C. 10:2b, 3a) but this call was limited for the time (D. and C. 10:8a). What was the nature of this limitation? Why was it imposed? Discuss the relation between preparation and magnifying one's calling.
7. Discuss the relation between gifts and responsibility. What varied consequences follow failure to "exercise" the gifts of God and to "magnify" one's calling? Is responsibility escapable?

8. Discuss the importance of the guidance of the Holy
   Spirit as indicated in these early revelations
   (D. and C. 6:7; 10:6, 7, 9, 10; 24:2c).

Exploration 10

APOSTOLIC MINISTRY

PREPARATORY READING: *New Commentary*, **pages 90-94**

ADDITIONAL BOOKS NEEDED: Church History, Volume 1; Doctrine and Covenants; Bible

Introduction

The primary need for apostolic witness was in the heart and mind of Joseph before the church was organized. By making it the special concern of the Presidency and Twelve, who are apostles, it was intended that as the church grows its life shall always center in this witness.

For Consideration

The revelation of June 1829 (D. and C. 16) looked toward the organization of the church and anticipated its worldwide growth. The basic requirement placed on all who would participate was that they would take upon themselves the name of Christ (D. and C. 16:4e, 5a, b). Note how closely this parallels the communion covenant (D. and C. 17:22d, 23b).

This revelation was given about ten months before the church was organized. Note the confidence with which universal evangelism was forecast (D. and C. 16:5a, b), its address to "every creature" and to all "who have arrived to the years of accountability" (D. and C. 16:5b, 6d).

Although Joseph Smith quite probably had much to

do with the selection and commissioning of the Twelve in 1835, the burden of this responsibility was placed on Oliver Cowdery, David Whitmer, and Martin Harris, who were the chief Book of Mormon witnesses. The apostles chosen by them were likewise to be "special witnesses" (D. and C. 16:61). The choice was not hurried. It took nearly six years to "search out" those called. The searching apparently culminated in observation of the abilities and conduct of the elders who were members of Zion's Camp (Church History, Volume 1, pages 540-541).

Although a new and distinctive movement was about to be initiated and this revelation was preparatory to its world outreach, ministers were told to "contend against no church save it be the church of the devil" (D. and C. 16:4d). Their message was to be affirmative. Opposition was not to be directed against established organizations (many of which were doing much good) but against teaching which misrepresented the truth as it is in Christ Jesus (John 8:39-44).

The apostolic mission looked toward the baptism (life commitment) of those who repented (D. and C. 16:5c). Baptism is an important social witness of repentance and involves both the individual and group. It is pointed toward the building of the kingdom (New Commentary, pages 92-93).

The Twelve could not take their personal witness into all the world. Their testimony must kindle the spirit of witness so that others would come to share this testimony and could then be called and commissioned (D. and C. 16:5e). Note in this connection Luke 10:1-2 and II Timothy 2:2.

The foundation of effective evangelism is worship (D. and C. 16:6c). The testimony must not go forth "in word only, but also in power, and in the Holy Ghost, and in much assurance" (I Thessalonians 1:5). The counterpart of sound worship is full commitment made strong in obedience (D. and C. 16:7). Witnesses must live according to their testimony. Since Jesus is the anointed of God, he has a right to command.

Questions and Discussion Topics

1. Do you regard the revelation setting forth the calling of the Twelve so long before the quorum was organized an indication ot the fundamental importance of their central task? Explain your answer.
2. How does the choice of the three witnesses to "search out the Twelve" seem especially suitable? What principles guided their search?
3. Discuss the meaning of the command, "Take upon you the name of Christ."
4. What is the basic apostolic task? Is this reserved to the Twelve alone? If not, who else shares it? In what way do you share this task?
5. What did the admonition to "contend against no church, save it be the church of the devil" (D. and C. 16:4d) mean in 1830? Now?
6. State the relation between repentance, baptism, and endurance.
7. Evangelism involves "the convincing of many of their sins, that they may come unto repentance" (D. and C. 16:7b). Many people today tend to

avoid soul-searching concern about sin—its rebellion against God, its flaunting of God's love, its betrayal of others. How does this affect the quality of repentance? See the *New Commentary*, page 94.

8. Oliver Cowdery and David Whitmer were never members of the Twelve, but are called "apostles" (D. and C. 16:3b; 17:1b; 83:10b). What other ministers are apostles? (D. and C. 139:1b, 145:3, 148:2). The members of what quorums are special assistants of the apostles? Who are the members of the Twelve today? When were they selected?

Exploration 11
EARLY EVANGELISM

PREPARATORY READING: *New Commentary*, **pages
79-84, 107, 155-157**
**ADDITIONAL BOOKS NEEDED: Doctrine and
Covenants**

Introduction

A dominant note of the early records of revelations
was the importance of personal testimony. Even when
regularly organized missionary journeys came to be
undertaken, the prevailing emphasis was still on
personal testimony rather than on formal preaching.

For Consideration

Many an early convert accepted the invitation to
"thrust in his sickle with his might, and reap while
the day lasts" (D. and C. 6:2; 4:1; 10:2; 30:1; 35).
Evangelism was not the task of a few but the privilege
of all. The church grew because of testimony borne to
families and friends. Most of the new members in the
church even today are the results of such testimony.

The early evangelism of the church was purposive.
It was to "bring forth and establish the cause of
Zion" (D. and C. 6:3; 10:3; 12:3). This was part of
the missionary message. It set the pattern of early
church life.

A further note in the early evangelism of the church
was the call to repentance (D. and C. 6:4; 12:4b;
13:3; 18:2). There was no conflict between these

emphases. Zion is the process of creative repentance.

A major source of the power in testimony of the Saints of the early Restoration was their conviction that the "field" was indeed "white already to harvest" (D. and C. 4:1c; 6:2a; 10:2a). Many were looking for such a message as the missionary brought, for God had prepared the way (D. and C. 34:2). This is as true today as it was in the 1830s.

The identical revelations given to John and Peter Whitmer in June 1829 (D. and C. 13, 14) set forth what would be of greatest worth to them. The need for repentance which they were to declare has to do with a sound attitude toward God. To adopt this attitude is fundamental. Elaboration of its resultant requirements would come within the fellowship of the Saints.

Note the deep satisfaction which the early missionaries were promised they would find in testimony (D. and C. 16:3f; 18:5f; 6b; 26:3d; 30:2a) and the incentives to personal righteousness they shared for the sake of this testimony.

Oliver and David were told to "remember the worth of souls is great in the sight of God" (D. and C. 16:3c). Disciples agree to this in a general fashion. What justified its mention in the revelation is the importance of this remembrance to witnesses of the Lord Jesus. It must determine their approach, their cultivation of missionary skills, their persistence.

Note the importance of remembrance in the lives of the Saints (D. and C. 16:3c). There are primary and derived areas of remembrance for disciples (D. and C. 17:22, 23).

Questions and Discussion Topics

1. What values accrued to the Saints themselves from their missionary testimony in their families? Among their friends?

2. What were the major emphases in the testimony of the early Saints? Are these emphases valid today? Should the content of the missionary message be fundamentally different from the content in the early days of the Restoration? If so at what point? Why?

3. Comment on the note of urgency evident in the command to the elders to thrust in their sickles with their might (D. and C. 4:1d; 11:2a), with their soul (D. and C. 30:2d), and with all their might, mind, and strength (D. and C. 32:2c). How does this urgency still exist? What should individual church members do about this?

4. Doctrine and Covenants 16:2a says that "the world is ripening in iniquity" and continues: "It must needs be that the children of men are stirred up unto repentance." What is the relative costliness of ill will between members of a family and between nations? In what way does the need for repentance parallel the breaking down of the barriers which up until now have divided people?

5. Oliver and David were told to "remember the worth of souls." Consider how such remembrance is related to the ordinances of the gospel, frequency of prayer, and content of prayer (D. and C. 17:22, 23; 4:2; 59:2h; 119:6c; and *New Commentary*, page 107).

6. What reason do today's disciples have for believing

that "the field is white already to harvest"? Why is it important to have such a conviction?

7. The instruction concerning the call to bear witness of the "great and marvelous work" which was "about to come forth" was given before offices in the priesthood were differentiated. When such differentiation was made, did it relieve those not members of the missionary quorums from the call to testify? If not, what difference did it make? (See D. and C. 38:9d; 85:22a.)

8. What major beliefs do the Saints hold in common with other Christians? Name important "Restoration distinctives." Should either be eliminated from our testimony? What would be the result if either was eliminated? In what spirit should distinctives be discussed?

Exploration 12

THE ORGANIZATION OF THE CHURCH

PREPARATORY READING: *New Commentary*, pages 94-108; Church History, Volume 1, pages 1-3, 34-40, 67-79

ADDITIONAL BOOKS NEEDED: Doctrine and Covenants

Introduction

The organization of the church was preceded by years of preparation during which Joseph grew in understanding. The faith and structure of the church took shape in his heart and mind. He shared it with Oliver and a few others. Much of what Joseph had learned was embodied in Doctrine and Covenants 17.

For Consideration

The idea that the restoration of the gospel was needed had been voiced by religious leaders such as Martin Luther, Roger Williams, John and Charles Wesley, and Alexander Campbell. The problem of many of Joseph's contemporaries was with the choice of such a man as he to become the spokesman of God to his generation, with the authority of the priesthood, and with the idea of current revelation.

There was nothing parochial about the outlook of the charter members of the church. They were entering on an enterprise which they believed would reach across the world and be of eternal significance. Although the organization of the church had been anticipated for a considerable time (D. and C. 4:1a; 5:3d; 10:8b), it did not take place until the "precise day" for organization was made known "by the spirit of prophecy and revelation" (D. and C. 17:Introduction). Note the importance of the preceding period of preparation and of the restraint practiced by Joseph during this period. Ten years elapsed between the date of the first vision and the organization of the church.

Note the authority underlying the organization of the church (D. and C. 17:1). The church was organized "agreeable to the laws of our country." The laws of the state of New York required that not less than six persons participate in such an organization. It is also interesting to note that over thirty persons were present at the time. Action was taken "by the will and commandments of God." The organization was "according to the grace of our Lord and Savior Jesus Christ." Joseph presided by virtue of the authority given him of God, but was required to secure the consent of the other participants in the organization before doing so (Church History, Volume 1, pages 76-77).

Doctrine and Covenants 17 is "a compilation of instructions received from time to time in connection with the organization of the church" (Introduction in Doctrine and Covenants 17 and Church History, Volume 1, page 36). With six charter members no elaborate organization was possible or necessary, although it had been envisioned (D. and C. 16).

Further organization came with the growth of the church and the enlistment of capable ministers. Note the comment of Heman C. Smith in this connection (*New Commentary*, page 108). The later insertion of paragraphs 16 and 17 was consistent with the purpose of the section and appears to have given rise to no comment at the time (*New Commentary*, page 105).

The instruction that "the elders are to conduct the meetings as they are led by the Holy Ghost, according to the commandments and revelations of God" (D. and C. 17:9), and that members of the Aaronic priesthood should do so only in the absence of the elders (D. and C. 17:10; 11c) implies no disregard of the dignity of the Aaronic priesthood. It emphasizes, rather, the importance of the presiding function and of the orderly promotion of the church purpose under the guidance of the Holy Spirit.

The functions of conferences have changed with the growth of the church and the clearer perception of the difference between the legislative, administrative, and judicial aspects of church government. The statement of President Joseph Smith III (*New Commentary*, pages 107-108) was issued a hundred years ago. Give thought to the permanent value of conferences and the ways in which some of the non-legislative values mentioned by President Smith may be preserved.

The inclusion in Doctrine and Covenants 17 of instructions concerning conference, ministerial licenses, approval of ordinations, and transfers is a good indication of the breadth of the expectations of the early Saints. In connection with the transfers it should be noted that a good recording system can be of great value to the church. It depends, almost entirely, on the faithfulness of officials charged with supplying the original data on such events as blessings, baptisms, and ordinations. But records are only tools. They demand study and interpretation, e.g., as a means of understanding fluctuations in baptismal rates.

Questions and Discussion Topics

1. What prior preparation had been made for the organization of the church? Why did the organization take place when it did? By what authority was the church organized?
2. Give a brief account of the service at which the church was organized. What principles guided the actions taken? Note the place of the principle of common consent (Church History, Volume 1, pages 76-77) and its extension to local organizations (D. and C. 17:16).
3. Joseph and Oliver were called to be apostles and the first and second elders of the church (D. and C. 17:1b). Later the revelation states that "an apostle is an elder." Does this imply that all elders have apostolic functions even though they are not members of the apostolic quorums? How? Why is this significant? (See New Commentary, page 101.)
4. Why was not the priesthood structure of the church set forth more fully in the first few months of the life of the church? Under what circumstances did further priesthood development

take place? According to what principles are members of the priesthood ordained (D. and C. 17:12, 16)?

5. What areas of ministry are assigned to all members of the priesthood? What are the distinctive functions of priests, teachers, deacons?

6. Why are the elders given primary responsibility in presiding over church services? How can elders preside through delegations of leadership in conducting services?

7. What is meant by the legislative, administrative, and judicial arms of the church government? Where and by whom are legislative functions exercised? Name major areas of church administration and who functions in them. Who are charged with judicial responsibilities in the church?

8. Early conferences were similar to the town meetings of pioneer times in the United States. Those present were there "to do whatever church business [was] necessary to be done at the time" (D. and C. 17:13). Conferences and jurisdictional business meetings now operate in more distinctively legislative areas. What types of church business still require legislative approval (D. and C. 17:16; 120:2a)?

Exploration 13

THE RESTORATION FAITH
THE NATURE OF DIVINITY

PREPARATORY READING: *New Commentary*, **pages 94-95, 98-101, 107-110**

ADDITIONAL BOOKS NEEDED: Bible, Doctrine and Covenants

Introduction

The Restoration faith centers in our understanding of the nature and purpose of God as revealed in the life and ministry of the Lord Jesus Christ and the witness of the Holy Spirit. The essentials are set forth in Doctrine and Covenants 17 and 18. Related revelations are consistent with the teachings of the other scriptures and are fundamental.

For Consideration

The Restoration is built on certain revelatory happenings, the testimony of Joseph Smith and others who participated in them, and the accompanying witness of the Holy Spirit. Our faith is thus rooted in history and testimony. In light of this, note the fundamental importance of divine revelation as found in Doctrine and Covenants 17:2, 3.

Doctrine and Covenants 17:4-6 contains a concise summary of the Restoration faith concerning the Father, Son, and Holy Spirit. It is attested by "we, the elders of the church" (D. and C. 17:3d) and possibly

61

by others. But the manner in which assurance came
to them is not disclosed.

Emphasis on the immutability (unchangeability) of
God runs through the revelations (D. and C. 2:1;
17:2g, 4a; 76:1; 129:8d), but our awareness of the
meaning of God's steadfastness undergoes constant
refinement as we respond to our heavenly Father in
worship and in loving service. The manifestations of
unchanging, divine love constitute a steadily growing
call to repentance—to change toward Godlikeness.

When we affirm that God is "infinite and eternal,
from everlasting to everlasting" (D. and C. 17:4a), we
are concerned with the "abidingness" of divinity.
"His years never fail" (D. and C. 76:1c). Love and
holiness abide with God, and what endures in him
endures forever—mercy (Psalms 106:1; 107:1),
righteousness (Psalms 111:3; 112:3, 9), and truth
(Peter 1:25).

Salvation is a gift of God through Christ and the
transforming power of the Holy Spirit (D. and C.
17:5). We cannot earn this gift, nor is it conceivable
that God will withhold it from any who seek to know
and to serve him (D. and C. 85:16). To understand
this, it must be considered against a background of
both time and eternity (D. and C. 17:4, 6; 43:6).

Note the intimate relation between worship, love for
God, and acceptable service. Faith and power are
rooted in worship (D. and C. 17:4).

The Holy Spirit "beareth record of the Father and
of the Son" (D. and C. 17:5g). We know God through
Christ (Hebrews 1:1-2; Ephesians 1:3; I Peter 1:3-4).
But we do not enter into the fullness of this revelation

except as the Holy Spirit brings conviction to our souls (John 15:26; I Corinthians 12:3).

Christ the Lord is revealed as "Alpha and Omega" (D. and C. 18:1a). He is the "Alpha"—the beginning; before the creation of human beings in the divine image he expressed the divine intention in his own being. And he is "Omega"—the end, the goal of our creation.

Questions and Discussion Topics

1. Recount briefly the historical background of Section 17. What evidences taken from the section itself indicate that it is a compilation from several revelations?
2. The restoration is rooted in history. Here, as elsewhere, God declared himself for our salvation. How is the importance of special revelatory acts a foundation of faith?
3. Comment on the importance in the Christian life of confidence in the unchangeability of God—his unfailing mercy, ever present power.
4. What is worship (D. and C. 17:4)? Is worship an end in itself? Explain. In what ways does worship enrich faith? engender spiritual power? clarify Christian purposes?
5. What is the meaning of the statement that God created us "after his own image and in his own likeness" (D. and C. 17:4b)?
6. What is the importance of baptism in light of Doctrine and Covenants 17:7b-d?
7. What is the meaning of the two phrases: "fall from grace" and "endure to the end"? In light of the

foregoing what does "salvation" mean?

8. The revelation to Martin Harris given in March
   1830 begins, "I am Alpha and Omega" (D. and C.
   18:1a). This expression is evidently important, for
   it echoes the New Testament (Revelation 1:8, 21:6,
   22:13) and occurs in twelve other places in the
   Doctrine and Covenants. What does it mean to
   you?

Exploration 14

ELEMENTS OF THE FAITH

PREPARATORY READING: *New Commentary*, **pages 109-110; Doctrine and Covenants 3:14; 12:5; 17:18**

Introduction

In expressing their faith the early Saints used many of the words that were used by other Christians, but the content of these words was enriched by the influence of their distinctive beliefs. When they told of faith in God, for example, they had in mind the God and Father of our Lord Jesus Christ who made himself known to the Book of Mormon peoples and was again revealing his will in the Restoration. For this reason the early Saints' basic beliefs are best understood in their interrelationships.

For Consideration

Recognition of the Lordship of Jesus Christ is the essence of the restoration evangel. The purpose of the Book of Mormon, as stated in the introduction, is "the convincing of the Jew and Gentile that Jesus is the Christ, the Eternal God, manifesting himself into all nations." The centrality of Christ is affirmed again and again in the introductions and content of the revelations. Note in this connection the prayers used in consecrating the sacramental emblems.

The faith enjoined in writings found in the Book of Mormon and Doctrine and Covenants is the faith in God who inspires the "marvelous work and a wonder."

It is assured confidence that the purposes of our creation can be fulfilled only under the guidance of our heavenly Father. It is expressed in repentance and obedience (D. and C. 1:4d; 8:3d; 16:2, 17:18c).

Baptism is a lifetime commitment. Faithfulness to the baptismal covenant is essential to salvation. Failure to "endure to the end" (D. and C. 16:4e; 17:6a; 18) is like quitting in the middle of a race.

The elders "confirm those who are baptized into the church, by the laying on of hands for the baptism of fire and the Holy Ghost" (D. and C. 17:8c). Those thus confirmed have already been blessed of the Holy Spirit as they have matured in faith and repentance and have sought baptism. However the richest blessings of the Spirit are enjoyed as members of the body of Christ. As these blessings are experienced the faith which led to baptism is confirmed and emphasized.

To partake of the sacrament of the Lord's Supper is to remember our personal relationships with Christ Jesus. This is also symbolized in the covenant made in the ordinance of baptism and confirmation. We see an apparent comparison in the statement on the duties of members (D. and C. 17:18) and the prayers used in consecrating the sacramental bread and wine (D. and C. 17:22, 23).

Eternal judgment, endless punishment, eternal damnation, and related themes were the stock in trade of many of the revivalist preachers of the early years of the nineteenth century. In response to an inquiry from Martin Harris, Joseph gave a very beautiful and satisfying explanation of the meaning of "eternal" in this connection and something of the nature of eternal glory. The essence of this instruction is that the word "eternal" does not refer to timelessness so much as it does to divinity. God is endless. The punishment which is given from him is endless since it partakes of his nature. It is rooted in justice, administered in hope, and may be averted by repentance and obedience (D. and C. 18:2a-e).

The cause of Zion had been near to the hearts of the Saints from the very beginning. It has always been associated with renunciation of temporal riches as an end in themselves (D. and C. 6:3; 10:3). That this is not a condemnation of riches as such is clear from the later instruction that the order of gathering should be "firstly the rich and the learned, the wise and the noble" (D. and C. 58:3e).

Most of the biblical condemnations of covetousness are directed against the immoral desire for that which belongs to another. Note the depth of the instruction to Martin Harris, "thou shalt not covet thine own property" (D. and C. 18:3b, 6a).

Questions and Discussion Topics

1. Why must the message of the Restoration be grounded in recognition of the Lordship of Jesus Christ? What does this mean?
2. What do we mean by faith in God? In what ways is our faith related to our expectations of the kingdom? to our courage in face of adversity? to the sincerity of our worship?
3. What are the essential conditions of Christian baptism? Comment on their importance.

4. Those who have been baptized are to be "confirmed" by the elders. What does this mean? Discuss the prerequisites of confirmation mentioned in the revelation (D. and C. 17:18a).
5. Analyze the prayers used in consecrating the emblems in the communion service. For whom are these emblems blessed? For what purpose are they partaken? What is the meaning of the expression "partake unworthily"?
6. What is the meaning of justification, sanctification, eternal judgment, and eternal life? See the *New Commentary*, pages 109-110, for help on these comments. Also define these words from your dictionary.
7. Why are we commanded to "seek not for riches but for wisdom"? Comment on the importance of wisdom in the management of all types of riches.
8. Discuss the meaning of covetousness. What is its relation to the management of one's own property?

Exploration 15
THE PLACE OF JOSEPH

PREPARATORY READING: *New Commentary,* **pages 97, 111-114, 131-132, 135, 188-191, 256-258, 320-322, 438; Doctrine and Covenants 17:1; 19:1-3; 27; 29:2d; 43:1-3; 67; 87:2, 3, 5; 122:2**

ADDITIONAL BOOKS NEEDED: Bible

Introduction

Joseph naturally took the place of leadership when the church was organized, but his relations with the other members of the church had to be worked out in changing situations. The major revelatory experiences concerning this were received during the first year of our church organization. However, expansions and modifications occurred from time to time as indicated.

For Consideration

Joseph functioned as a prophet before the church was organized (D. and C. 4; 6; 10). On April 6, 1830, he became the prophet-leader of the church. His call to declare the will and purpose of God now merged into his calling to lead the Saints toward becoming a prophetic people.

The Church of Jesus Christ is a new creation, influenced by God's Spirit, and restoring by the mandate of God. It is more than an association of persons in order to achieve religious purposes more advantageously. It is a living body, possessed of insight and great people, and dedicated to a great cause. The Spirit of the Lord Jesus was with the prophet and his associate ministers according to the gifts and callings of God. The Spirit ministered to them and through them. Thus the church became enlightened and empowered as the bearer of a living testimony.

To function effectively, the prophet walks "in all holiness before God." It is to the guidance thus received that the Saints must "give heed. . . in all patience and faith" (D. and C. 19:2a-b). Note the importance of holiness in this connection. It has to do with character. Love and holiness are the two ultimate characteristics of divinity.

Joseph, and only Joseph, was appointed to "receive commandments and revelations in this church" (D. and C. 27:2a). The key word here is "appointed." The prophet is chosen by God. The church does not elect him, but recognizes and honors the call of God. Others may be endowed with the spirit of the prophets but do not function for the church as a whole (Revelation 19:10).

Acceptance of the divine direction given through the prophet is not a passive affair. The "common consent" required (D. and C. 27:4c) is more than "common assent." It is known at its best when approached "by the prayer of faith" of those who, like the prophet, "walk in all holiness" before God (D. and C. 19:2a).

The kingdom of God reflects the nature of God. We cannot imagine either a lesser or a greater purpose in creation than kingdom building. God is involved and will not be satisfied with anything less. A function of prophetic ministry is to promote the cause of Zion in the power of the Almighty (D. and C. 19:2d).

There are different levels of prophetic guidance even in the Doctrine and Covenants. A revelation indicating that a certain person shall occupy in a certain place is important. This is not nearly so important against the background of eternity as further disclosure of the nature of divinity or further definition of the character and purpose of God's kingdom.

Revelation invites judgment. Some of the early Saints were critical of the word received through Joseph, but were reassured after W. E. McClellin failed to produce an acceptable counterpart. The ultimate test was not the words used but spiritual quality (D. and C. 67:2d).

Questions and Discussion Topics

1. By what authority did Joseph Smith preside at the organization of the church? By what action was this authority augmented at the charter meeting?
2. Comment on the meaning of the titles applied to Joseph: Apostle, Seer, Translator, Prophet. How are these titles still applicable to the president of the church?
3. How is the church an organism rather than an organization? How does its parts enrich by adding to each other and uniting the life of the body?
4. In what attitude must the prophet seek divine guidance? How does the quickening of his

intelligence prepare him for this guidance? Why? In what ways can the Saints support the prophet most effectively?

5. What is the responsibility of the Saints toward the word received through the prophet? Explain what was involved in the instruction that Joseph should be appointed to preside over the conference "by the voice of it," and that "all things must be done in order and by common consent in the church, by the prayer of faith" (D. and C. 27:4a-c).

6. Why do we sustain the president of the church, and no one else, as prophet? Does this mean that he, and no other, may rightly exercise the gift of prophecy among the Saints? Why? Why not?

7. What is the ultimate test of the validity of a prophetic message? What bearing does the ministry of the Holy Spirit have at this point?

8. What provision is made for succession in the prophetic office? What is required of such a successor (D. and C. 43:1-2)?

Exploration 16

EMMA SMITH AND THE WOMEN OF ZION

PREPARATORY READING: *New Commentary*, **pages 124, 294-296; Church History, Volume 1, pages 119-122; Volume 2, pages 339, 571-572; Volume 3, page 506; Doctrine and Covenants 24, 82;** *Emma Smith* **by Margaret Wilson Gibson, Herald House, 1966**

Introduction

The pioneer women of the early church were primarily concerned with homes and children, the support of the ministry, and such aids as social service and the improvement of the quality of church life. Emma Smith, wife of Joseph, was a natural leader.

For Consideration

Home building and maintenance on the frontier in the 1830s and 1840s was an arduous task. Much of the burden fell on the women and these showed intense interest in the health and education of their children. Schools were among the first buildings to be erected (D. and C. 55:2). There was dedication underlying the willingness of Emma Smith and others to move from the relatively settled eastern states to face the hardships of the frontier.

Note the strictness of the command to show the Book of Mormon plates only to those chosen to be witnesses and the acceptance of this restriction by Emma. She was aware of the plates since she served for a time as scribe for Joseph (Church History, Volume 3, pages 355-358).

Emma Smith was ordained by Joseph to expound scriptures and to exhort the church. This was part of her office and calling (D. and C. 24:2a-c). Years later, in discussing his blessing by his father in Liberty Jail, Joseph Smith III wrote, "This blessing has by some been called an ordination, from the usual predilection to confound names and terms" (Church History, Volume 3, page 506). The "ordination" of Emma may have been of similar nature. It did involve a call and a promise of power even though no priesthood office appears to have been involved.

Emma was called to "make a selection of sacred hymns" and did so. The hymns selected had been written, before the church was organized, by authors who knew nothing of the Restoration. Such "qualified dependence upon their Gentile neighbors" was both profitable and inescapable even though the Saints were admonished "to be in the world but not of it" (D. and C. 128:8a, b).

Emma was also called to be a "comfort" to Joseph in his afflictions, with consoling words, in a spirit of meekness" (D. and C. 24:2a). There is no hint of subservience here. "Meekness" refers to power controlled in quietness. That which was Emma's freely chosen privilege and duty was to be recognized as her gift and calling under God.

The revelations given to the church in the early days of the Restoration lay great stress on the importance of the home and family (D. and C. 17:10b, 68:4a-c; 87:5e; 90:6d-9). The importance of family life and ministries continues today.

The basic law of the church says that a husband shall love his wife with all his heart (D. and C. 42:7d). Consider this in terms of acting lovingly toward one's spouse whatever the provocation to do otherwise (Matthew 5:46-48).

A fundamental kingdom concern is for the welfare of the needy. The instruction in Doctrine and Covenants 82 makes this ministry a specific charge against the Lord's storehouse which must be maintained as the duty and privilege of stewards. Affirmation of this principle was a needed assurance provided by Doctrine and Covenants 82. Contributions to the oblation fund, as well as the general payment of tithes, should be regarded from this vantage point.

Questions and Discussion Topics

1. Under what condition was Emma promised an inheritance in the cause of Zion? Why was she especially concerned about this at this time? Discuss, briefly, the nature of her partnership with her husband.

2. What were the specific things which Emma had not seen and which are referred to in Doctrine and Covenants 24? Discuss the principle involved in the command, "Murmur not because of the things which thou hast not seen."

3. In what sense was Emma an "elect lady"? Name

some others to whom such a title might well be applied.

4. What special task was given to Emma in this revelation? When was it fulfilled? What obligations were involved? In what way does Emma's influence reach to our own times?
5. Emma was "ordained" to exercise what functions? Who else is commissioned to similar functions? Did Emma's "ordination" involve priesthood?
6. Comment on other major contributions which Emma Smith made to the life of the church. Of what particular contribution are we the beneficiaries today?
7. Briefly enumerate the instructions of the church concerning widows and orphans (D. and C. 82). What bearing do these instructions have on godly family life?
8. What are the provisions of the church for the protection of the families of deceased stewards? Is the law in this regard still operative? What is the obligation of other stewards in this connection?

Exploration 17

ANTICIPATIONS OF ZION

PREPARATORY READING: *New Commentary,* **pages 134, 143, 157-158, 161-162, 165-167, 171; Doctrine and Covenants 27:3; 28:2; 30:3; 36; 38:4, 7, 9; 45:12-13**

ADDITIONAL BOOKS NEEDED: Bible

Introduction

The cause of Zion was dear to the hearts of the Saints from the very beginning. It was a dominant factor in determining the methods and content of their missionary work. This cause shaped the lives of the converts after baptism. The members looked forward eagerly to the designation of a place of gathering so they could be the living ensign.

For Consideration

A year before the church was organized Oliver Cowdery was commanded to "seek to bring forth and establish the cause of Zion." This instruction was repeated shortly thereafter to Hyrum Smith, Joseph Knight, and David Whitmer (D. and C. 6:3; 10:3; 11:3; 12:3). Soon after the church was organized Joseph was told: "Thou shalt devote all thy service in Zion. And in this thou shalt have strength" (D. and C. 23:4a). What is the place of the cause of Zion in the message and ministries of the church?

The early revelations anticipated the gathering of the Saints "into one place" on the American frontier

(D. and C. 27:3d; 28:2d). The attempts to gather could not be sustained. Nor have the calamities foretold in Doctrine and Covenants 1:4; 28:4-6; 45:8 or by the ancient prophets (Malachi 4:1) yet taken place. It will be helpful to consider, however, the calamitous nature of modern life in terms of God's purpose. Think of the revelation which would come to the world from a strong and righteous people.

The situation of a godly people in a "land of promise" (D. and C. 38:4d) is a recurring theme of the scriptures. The "promise" of any land depends on the quality of its people, their caliber, their relation to each other and to God.

No mere change of location can provide a sound foundation for Zion. With this in mind note the importance of preparing for the gathering (D. and C. 28:2d; 58:3b; 65).

We are not alone in our concern for Zion. Zionic endeavor is sustained by the Spirit. This is to be expected, since the process of being the kingdom by the free choice and joint action of the disciples is the goal set for us by God. If we tend to become discouraged we should count our allies (D. and C. 36:6, 12; 38:9).

The spirit of the gathering is of primary importance. Note in this connection that the Saints moved to Ohio to escape the power of the enemy but also to be "gathered unto me a righteous people" (D. and C. 38:7a). Finding a congenial environment is important, but only as it ministers to godliness. The relationship of people is of primary importance, not location.

78

The gathering to Kirtland was not intended to be final. The Saints had already been told that their city would be "on the borders by the Lamanites" (D. and C. 27:3d). But it proved to be an important place of preparation. In similar fashion many practical lessons of importance to the kingdom may be learned wherever Saints regard church membership as a commitment to fellowship in righteousness.

The symbolism of the move to Ohio, with the prospect of a later move to the still more distant frontier, quite probably appealed to many of the Saints. They were engaged in a dramatic portrayal of the meaning of repentance, leaving a way of life which had hitherto seemed good to them and risking all on their faith that God was beckoning them to a life of even greater worth (Hebrews 11:14-16).

Questions and Discussion Topics

1. Why did the early Saints find the idea of a gathering so attractive? What were the major reasons for gathering mentioned in the revelations?
2. What bearing did the prophecy of Enoch have on the understanding of the Saints of the nature of Zion? on the age-long concern of the people of God to build cities of righteousness?
3. Discuss the bearing of the principles of the gospel on the building of the kingdom. Note the importance of the preparation of the hearts of the disciples for effective kingdom building (D. and C. 28:2d; 31:1a; 38:4e; 58:3b).
4. What were the Saints seeking as they moved into Ohio and looked forward to the move farther

west? How were their expectations realized?
disappointed? refined?

5. What is the meaning of "the cause of Zion"? How
is our understanding of this cause growing
sounder? What factors make for the refinement of
our understanding?

6. What is the relation of sacrifice to the
establishment of Zion? To whom is genuine Zionic
achievement worth the sacrifices entailed?

7. What makes any land a "land of promise"? one
with high promise?

8. What is the importance of the doctrine of the
gathering in the life of the church today? How is it
more than fleeing in a time of crisis? In what ways
can we gather wherever the church is found?
Today's church has centers throughout the world.
How are they centers for Zionic gathering?

Exploration 18

SOBERNESS, URGENCY, JUDGMENT

PREPARATORY READING: *New Commentary,* **pages
190-191, 194-196, 314-315; Doctrine and Covenants
43:5-8; 45:1-10; 85:24-25**

ADDITIONAL BOOKS NEEDED: Bible

Introduction

The early Saints shared with others of their times
and with disciples of earlier generations a deep
conviction that God is working out his purposes in
history. Contemplation of the certainty of judgment
and of the early return of the Lord Jesus Christ
sustained in them a sense of serious and sober
purpose. They were "anxiously engaged in a good
cause" (D. and C. 58:6d).

For Consideration

The early Saints found sources of joy which were
not incompatible with deep seriousness (D. and C.
6:14; 10:7; 16:3, 4). It was in this spirit that they
were admonished to welcome to their assemblies those
who were "earnestly seeking the kingdom" (D. and C.
46:2, 3a).

This deep seriousness was directly related to a
pervasive note of urgency. They thought of themselves
as "latter day" Saints. This empowered many of their
sacrifices.

The note of urgency found in the revelations and
echoed in the lives of many of the Saints stressed the

importance of the present as their day of opportunity (D. and C. 45:1, 2, 6). Note the warning sounded recently in this connection (D. and C. 142:5b).

The seriousness and the sense of urgency of the Saints were also related to their conviction of eternal judgment. They saw judgment as written into the scheme of things. Every catastrophe should remind of the maladjustments which went before while every victory should impress the importance of the preparation which preceded it. In nature and in human nature, in time and in eternity, the crop is determined by the kind of seed that is sown and the way it is nurtured (D. and C. 43:5-6; Galatians 6:7-8). Contemplation of the principle of eternal judgment quickened in the Saints a conviction of victory (D. and C. 6:3; 12:5c; 58:6d-e). They trusted God for vindication of their faith and life (D. and C. 42:12d-f; 58:1-2).

Belief in the return of Jesus Christ is scriptural (Acts 1:9-11), but we do not have to wait for the return of Christ. The soundest guarantee of his coming is in our experience of his presence now. Note the word to Orson Pratt: "If you are faithful, behold *I am with you* until I come" (D. and C. 33:2b).

While the Saints of the early Restoration were convinced that the return of the Lord Jesus "with power and great glory" was near at hand (D. and C. 28:2g), a careful reading of the scriptures indicates that the great question is not when the Son of Man shall come, or when the great and culminating judgment of God shall be poured out upon the earth, but how fully the Saints will be prepared to participate in these great events when they do occur. The great question is, "When the Son of Man cometh, shall he find faith on the earth?" (See Luke 18:8.)

Questions and Discussion Topics

1. Consider the meaning of the instruction to Oliver Cowdery to "perform with soberness the work which I have commanded you" and that to the three Book of Mormon witnesses to "speak the truth in soberness" (D. and C. 6:16b; 16:4e). Note the relation of this instruction to the importance of a serious life purpose.

2. What were the roots of the urgency demonstrated in the lives of the early Saints? How did such urgency characterize the lives of the Saints of the first century (Mark 1:12-13; Matthew 4:16-22; Philippians 3:14-21)? In what way can it be quickened among us?

3. How did the pioneers of the Restoration express their sense of urgency in their preaching, in their testimony, and in their sacrificial commitment?

4. How do natural events illustrate the working of the principle of cause and effect? What is the relation of coming events to our present way of living? In what fashion does awareness of judgment constitute a constructive invitation to repentance?

5. How is eternal judgment a principle of promise, a justification of faith in God?

6. How is faith in the return of the Lord Jesus as shown in present endowment of his Spirit a reason for living with joyous purpose?

7. Many believers have felt sure that the return of

Jesus Christ is at hand. Is concern over the time of his return of primary importance? Why? If not, what is?

8. How is the foundation of Zion part of the worship of the Saints?

Exploration 19
THE BASIC LAW: PRINCIPLES

PREPARATORY READING: *New Commentary*, **pages 173-174; 177-178; 183-187; Doctrine and Covenants 12; 18; 20:23, 41; 42:1-3, 6-9**
ADDITIONAL BOOKS NEEDED: Bible; Church History, Volume 1

Introduction

The move to Kirtland, where nearly a hundred members had been baptized, gave the church an opportunity to consolidate the rather fragmentary organization of the New York period. As instructed, the elders met together in the spirit of prayer and were given what has proved to be one of the most important revelations in the Doctrine and Covenants. Under its terms the work at Kirtland grew until the small, incomplete, and preliminary organization effected at Fayette, New York, merged into the church with its quorums and councils provided for in the law.

For Consideration

The elders who were in Kirtland carried over from their earlier groupings (Disciples, Shakers, and others) strongly held opinions concerning church organization, the social obligations of believers, and similar matters. It was important that they all meet together in faith and in the spirit of prayer "to agree" concerning the beliefs and basic structure of the church in light of the enlarged understanding they had now received (D. and C. 41:1b). Apparently their efforts toward agreement were blessed (D. and C. 42:1c).

In harmony with Doctrine and Covenants 17:1, Joseph Smith and Oliver Cowdery were already recognized as the first and second elders of the church. Elder Edward Partridge, who was now called to be the bishop of the church, was described by Joseph Smith as "one of the heads of the church" (Church History, Volume 1, page 170). That he was called this early (D. and C. 41:3c-d), prior to other general officers, gives some indication of the importance of temporalities in the early church.

The first commandment given the elders was that they should go forth in the name of Christ and in the power of his Spirit to preach the principles of the gospel (D. and C. 42:2, 5). The necessity for this was obvious at the time. What is equally vital, though perhaps less obvious, is that the church of tomorrow depends on the effective evangelism of today.

The ministry of the elders was (is) to be conducted on a foundation of faith and prayer. This has to do with both content and spirit. It applies to the ministry of others also—both priesthood and non-priesthood. It is beyond belief that the Lord will refuse to grant his Spirit to those who seek it with all their hearts, so that this requirement calls for the unfailing observance of "prayers before the Lord in the season thereof" (D. and C. 68:4h).

Even the Saints are sinners (Romans 3:23; 5:12;

I John 1:7-9). We need to recognize this in humility and in the spirit of repentance. But it is unrepented sin which cuts us out from the fellowship of the people of God. This is true whether our sin is known to others or not (D. and C. 42:7, 11).

Repentance centers in adjustment to the will of God. The will to repent grows out of the sincere and continuing worship of God. The ethical requirements of sainthood may be catalogued in a code of laws but, essentially, they denote areas of response to the love of God (D. and C. 42:8a; 147:5a).

In certain areas, the healing ministry is primarily the concern of the elders (D. and C. 42:12, 13). But healing in the larger sense is the concern of all disciples. Note the healing ministries which are born of the Holy Spirit in the fellowship of the saints (Galatians 5:22-26).

In the Sermon on the Mount, Jesus taught that those against whom a brother has cause for complaint must first attempt to become reconciled before their gifts will be acceptable (Matthew 5:23-24). Note the attempt suggested in Doctrine and Covenants 42:23 to keep the reconciliation of differences within the smallest possible circle.

Questions and Discussion Topics

1. The church was commanded to support the elders at Kirtland when they met in faith and prayer "to agree." Comment on this in connection with the spirit of the legislative assemblies of the church. What is the bearing of this principle on the occasional practice of the prior instruction of

delegates to World Conferences?
2. Note the qualifications which Edward Partridge brought to his calling as bishop (D. and C. 41:2b-3d). Comment on their importance to the church in light of Doctrine and Covenants 42:8-9.
3. The two-by-two principle in evangelism, stated early in the experience of the church, was restated from time to time in revelations given through Joseph Smith, Jr. (D. and C. 52:3c; 60:3a; 61:6b; 62:2b) and renewed in 1863 (D. and C. 115:1c-d) and in 1925 (D. and C. 135:4). What values recommend this procedure?
4. Enumerate values which accrued to the church and to those participating through the practice of evangelism.
5. What are the benefits of regular personal and family prayer? How is there a connection between prayer and evangelism? How does it improve and empower the lives of the Saints? How do our lives witness? What does this say about a decrease in baptism? How can this trend be reversed?
6. Many of us regulate our ethical conduct according to the standards of our times and communities. Do the standards set in Doctrine and Covenants 42 require something better of us than this? Explain. What are our major resources for such improvement as is reasonably required?
7. Enumerate some of the healing ministries available in the church. By whom can these be exercised? What ministry can the church bring to disciples who are sick but who lack faith to be healed (D. and C. 42:12c, 13b)?

8. A few years ago, in a Communion service, a member of the church stated that he could not partake because he could not forgive another who had done him a great disservice. Afterward these reactions were expressed: (a) that he was right; he should refrain, for he would "partake unworthily" if he did so before forgiving the offender; and (b) in view of his own daily transgressions and his continuing need of God's forgiveness, he should have sought reconciliation with his brother, and having done so, he should partake. Discuss these reactions and any others which seem pertinent to this situation.

Exploration 20

THE BASIC LAW: STEWARDSHIP

PREPARATORY READING: *New Commentary*, **pages 171-174, 179-184**

ADDITIONAL BOOKS NEEDED: Bible, Doctrine and Covenants

Introduction

From the beginning of the movement the Saints recognized individual responsibilities as stewards (D. and C. 18:3). With the move to Kirtland, more specific instruction was needed concerning the principles and implementation of stewardship within the group.

For Consideration

The distribution of wealth proposed in this revelation is not primarily a social affair but a spiritual affair. Its motivation is, "If thou lovest me." If this basic impulse is removed, we have no guarantee of the effective reorganization of society. Kingdom building fails in its objective except as it is motivated by the pure love of God.

The instruction to accumulate surplus which "shall be kept in my storehouse" (D. and C. 42:10b; 122:6) is akin to the setting aside of gifts and the allocation of special appropriations by World Conferences. The oblation fund is an important special reserve. Note the recent instruction received concerning financing the building of the Temple out of contributions of surplus

90

(D. and C. 149:6; 149A:5).

Basic to stewardship is remembrance of the poor (D. and C. 42:8b). In the practice of stewardship we acknowledge the obligations which arise out of our kinship under God. Some obligations to the poor are glaringly apparent. Many who are poor need food, clothing, shelter, friends. These needs call for our ministry (Romans 12:20). But there are deeper levels of poverty. People need to share in truth, beauty, goodness, and the life abundant (John 10:10). These needs were among the concerns of Jesus. They must be ours (D. and C. 147:5a).

The command that the Saints shall not be idle (D. and C. 42:12b) goes hand in hand with the obligation to share (Galatians 6:2). The joys of creation are intended to find their counterpart in the joys of mutual helpfulness rather than in the satisfaction of individual appetites.

Obedience to the law in the field of temporalities requires responsible operation of the affairs of the steward as well as responsible accounting to the chosen representatives of God. Such management as stewards exercise seeks always to be efficient; but to struggle to match industrial efficiency, for example, with the promotion of spiritual well-being makes ever new and more searching demands.

Students of the word of God tell us that the basic and distinctive characteristics of our heavenly Father are love and holiness. Since we are called to make the practice of stewardship a searching and rewarding demonstration of our discipleship, this too must be characterized by pure and unblemished love for God and for all humankind.

Questions and Discussion Topics

1. Who are the poor? Does our answer tend to change with the enlargement of our own resources? Should it? Note in this connection the instruction to "the *principle* of sacrifice and repression of unneccessary wants" (D. and C. 130:7; 147:5a). To whom are these words addressed? How does this principle apply to today's economics?
2. Concern for the poor is expressed among the earliest of the revelations (D. and C. 34:4, 38:8). Removal of poverty was achieved, at least to a degree, under Enoch (D. and C. 36:2h-i). Comment on some of the creative demands the fight against poverty makes on the poor and on the well-to-do.
3. Why should stewards under God be concerned for the poor? What, if anything, can transform the concern of a steward from an obligation to a privilege? What are the rewards of such concern?
4. Urgent needs of the poor and oppressed call for aid even when no organized relief is readily available (Romans 12:20). Comment on this in relation to the support which Saints should give to relieve needs, both near and far, which the church cannot yet reach. What other organizations are assisting this activity of God? How are they reaching people we can't? How can we avoid duplication of effort?
5. Observance of the law of temporalities is best begun in family circles. Comment on the duties of parents in this connection (D. and C. 68:4). Consider in this connection, also, the kind of educational and caring ministry the priest needs to bring who is called to visit members and exhort

them to "attend to all family duties" (D. and C.
17:10b).

6. Note the purposes for which surplus is to be
gathered. In what way(s) may this be done "for
the salvation" of contributors (D. and C. 42:10c)?
For what purposes should surplus be distributed?
What obligations rest on those distributing? What
specific groups carry this responsibility in the
World Church? in stakes? in districts? How does
the principle of surplus apply in a Third World
country where many struggle just to survive?

Exploration 21

GIFTS OF THE SPIRIT

PREPARATORY READING: *New Commentary*, **pages 199-201, 206-208; Doctrine and Covenants 34:3; 42:13; 46:1b, 3b, c, 4a, 5, 7; 50:6b**

ADDITIONAL BOOKS NEEDED: Bible

Introduction

As the membership of the church grew, and as the Saints were blessed with diverse gifts of the Holy Spirit according to their several needs and capacities, it became necessary to have some recognized modes of procedure and some fundamental tests of the spiritual quality of their experiences. Here, as elsewhere, the guidance given them was related to their specific experiences, but the principles set forth are of permanent value.

For Consideration

The gifts of God to those who seek to serve are as numerous and as diverse as the disciples themselves. For purposes of instruction and explanation they are often grouped in categories as they are in some of the references listed here, but experiences of divine guidance and endowment are not restricted to these categories. The Spirit divides "to every man severally as he will" (I Corinthians 12:11).

Possibly the most evident and urgent need common to all the Saints was for such guidance in their services of worship as would make for order and light

94

and power. Some approximation of this might be achieved under the leadership of wise and able men and women, but more than this was needed. They needed the ministry of the Holy Spirit (D. and C. 46:1b).

Effectual seeking and exercising of the gifts of the Holy Spirit require of the disciple "holiness of heart," "walking uprightly," "considering the end of your salvation," and "doing all things with prayer and thanksgiving." The gifts of the gospel pertain to life in all its parts (D. and C. 46:3b, c).

All of us live in an atmosphere of partial understanding. Our lives are dedicated to the pursuit of clearer and sounder insights, but we are constantly distracted by the lure of lesser goods. We have available wisdom greater than our own to assist us in discerning what are the "best gifts" and why these are "best." Honest seekers grow under the guidance of the Holy Spirit and in sharing the benefits of the gifts enjoyed in the fellowship of the faithful.

Many have been greatly blessed by what have been called "the outward manifestations" of the gifts. These are among the gifts which we should "seek earnestly." But we should learn to appreciate, also, those quiet ministries of the Spirit by which some are brought to deeper conviction of the love of God, some to more grateful commitment to discipleship, and some to insight by which the unity of the body is augmented.

Although we are to "seek earnestly the best gifts," we must do so in humility. The "best gifts" are those our heavenly Father desires to give us. Many are already ours as potentials which we regard as our natural endowment. To make them—or others not so apparent—the "best gifts" requires that they shall be related to his purpose for us and for all others.

The elders were told, "That which does not edify is not of God" (D. and C. 50:6b). Edification has to do with building (as in erecting an edifice). One of the soundest tests we can apply to that which claims to come from God is to consider whether its effect is to edify. Read I Corinthians 14:3 in this light.

It is sometimes very helpful to think of the gifts of God to others as ways our lives are enriched. The artistry of a great musician, the creative impact of an able teacher, the dedicated financial judgment of those who labor to complete the half-fulfilled visions of our past are all gifts of faithful men and women without whose insights and services so many of us would have gone unblessed.

Questions and Discussion Topics

1. What do we mean by gifts of the Spirit? Name some of the categories in which these are listed in the scriptures. Name some other gifts which are mentioned in the scriptures but not in the categories already noted. Is there any limit to the number of gifts of the Spirit? Explain.
2. Why is it important that those leading the services of worship shall do so as they themselves are led by the Holy Spirit? What obligations does this place on them? On the congregation? In what ways does the Spirit lead those who plan the order of worship? sermons?

3. What is meant by prophecy? Does it mean foretelling or something more than this? What of the gift of discerning of spirits (Corinthians 12:10; D. and C. 46:7)? Under what circumstances is this gift especially important?
4. Discuss the meaning of the injunction given the Saints, "Seek ye earnestly the best gifts" (D. and C. 46:4a). Note (a) the slightly different phrasing of I Corinthians 14:11 and (b) the important addition to Doctrine and Covenants 46:4a. What is the connection of the Holy Spirit to the recommended seeking, coveting, and remembering? Why?
5. Enumerate some of the factors which determine the availability of gifts of the Spirit. Give thought to the causes and cost of overeagerness for specific gifts of the Spirit and of indifference to the gifts of the Spirit.
6. Name from your own experience ways in which you have experienced the ministry of the Holy Spirit when alone or in a small group, when in the fellowship of the Saints, and when studying the scriptures. Is it possible to receive such gifts without becoming aware of them? If so, why? If not, why not?
7. What steps may the Saints take to avoid deception in the matter of gifts of the Holy Spirit? What is the importance of edification in this connection?
8. Discuss ways in which the sound exercise of gifts of the Spirit has unified and enriched the fellowship of the Saints, e.g. the work of the great hymn writers, teachers, and others.

Exploration 22

GATHERING

PREPARATORY READING: *New Commentary*, **pages 185, 212-237**

ADDITIONAL BOOKS NEEDED: Doctrine and Covenants

Introduction

The first journey to Independence is a parable of our total church endeavor. The elders and priests who had enlisted in the cause of Zion went up to the promised land under divine direction, bearing testimony along the way. There was a comparatively small number of them. This made effective organization difficult. Much was learned and men with capacity for leadership moved to the fore.

For Consideration

Major factors prompting the move to Ohio now prompted the further migration to Missouri (D. and C. 38:7; 52:2a). The Saints sought to "escape the power of the enemy" and to build up "a righteous people."

The willingness of the Saints to undergo the hardships involved in the move to Missouri was due to more than their desire for a frontier location. They believed that here the kingdom of God was to be established. This conviction influenced all that they did (D. and C. 52:1b).

Not all the enemies of the Restoration were those opposed to their journeying to Independence. Some were members of the church who were as yet unwilling to make the sacrifices called for (D. and C. 54:1). This was never entirely overcome and had a great deal to do with the subsequent expulsion of the Saints from Missouri (D. and C. 98:1-3).

The elders went two-by-two, "preaching the word by the way" (D. and C. 52:3, 5, 6). They established important contacts along different routes between Kirtland and Missouri (D. and C. 52:7a). Many of them had prior ministerial experience and their forthright testimonies concerning fundamentals led to many conversions (D. and C. 52:3b; 18:4; 42:5). While those named went toward Missouri, the "residue of the elders" were to "watch over the churches" and also to "declare the word in the regions among them." Evangelism was the concern of the whole church (D. and C. 52:9).

Note that obedience to the ordinances is mentioned frequently (D. and C. 52:3c, 4c, 4d). The term "ordinances" is apparently used to refer to the commands of God as these pertain to all of life.

Note that men of goodwill and of more than ordinary capacity who joined the church were immediately assigned to places of major responsibility and became involved in the march toward Independence. In addition to those won earlier (Oliver Cowdery, the Whitmers, Sidney Rigdon, Edward Partridge) these included such men as T. B. Marsh (church physician, apostle), Sidney Gilbert (bishop's agent, storekeeper), W. W. Phelps (printer, editor, hymn writer), and others.

Throughout the early revelations runs a note of

concern for the poor. This is sound, but those possessing temporal means have an important part in kingdom building. In this connection note the order of gathering: "Firstly the rich and the learned, the wise and the noble" (D. and C. 58:3e). Note also the instruction given Sidney Gilbert (D. and C. 57:4a, b).

The denunciation of the rich who ignore the needs of the poor is not unexpected among such a company, but the denunciation of the ungodly poor is equally sound although, probably, less expected. Some who had gathered to Missouri had done so with less regard for the kingdom than for their own material well-being (D. and C. 56:5a-b).

Questions and Discussion Topics

1. What earlier experience of the Saints formed a helpful background for their move to Missouri? What specific preliminary work had been done before Joseph and the body of the Saints left for the West? When did Joseph and his company leave Kirtland? When did they reach Missouri?
2. Why was the doctrine of the gathering important to the early Saints? What did they hope to achieve? What part did the frontier play in their thinking?
3. What scriptural precedents probably influenced the thinking of the early Saints regarding the gathering? How may they have been influenced by more recent religiously motivated gatherings and by any contemporary movements of this nature?
4. Where were the most serious "enemies" of the Saints and the gathering to be found? Why are these enemies so important? How can they be

overcome? How long does it take to do this?

5. What instructions concerning their journey were given the elders who went to Missouri? What important results accrued from the manner of their travels? What instructions were given the elders who remained in Ohio?

6. On what principle were the first elders chosen to go to Missouri? Later a definite order of gathering was recommended. What was it? How sound was it? Why was it necessary?

7. What choices often confront rich people in such an enterprise as this? poor people? Which choices may have disadvantages? On what principle can these be turned into advantages?

8. When the early Saints gathered to Missouri what was their most valuable equipment? Why? Is this true of us? Explain.

Exploration 23

THE LAND OF ZION

PREPARATORY READING: *New Commentary*, pages 223-235

ADDITIONAL BOOKS NEEDED: Bible, Doctrine and Covenants

Introduction

The cause of Zion, although envisioned in part from the beginning, did not take clear and specific meaning until the Saints sought to plant the roots of the kingdom in Missouri. This was an enterprise of the utmost seriousness. It called for both temporal and spiritual disciplines. The example of the pioneer families should be an inspiration to all who follow.

For Consideration

Once it was so designated, Independence, Missouri, became the "Center Place" of the Restoration in more ways than one. For many it is both the focal point and the symbol of the kingdom.

The purpose and the expectations of the Saints who were gathering in Missouri were illustrated in the dedication of the land of Zion and of the "spot for the Temple." Each was important to the other.

The purchase of land and the location of the Saints were of primary practical importance as the settlement progressed in and around Independence. None of the things which had been planned could be done satisfactorily except as those involved had confidence in both the wisdom and the integrity of Bishop Edward Partridge and his close associate, Sidney Gilbert. The church was fortunate that when Joseph Smith returned to Kirtland Bishop Partridge was available to supervise both the temporal and spiritual activities of the community (D. and C. 58:15b).

Ownership of the land in and around Independence was of great importance to the Saints (D. and C. 57:1a; 58:7d, 10). Note that even this early the possibility of conflict was seen if the land was not purchased (D. and C. 58:11c).

The instruction that "it is not meet that I should command in all things" and that "men should be anxiously engaged in a good cause and do many things of their own free will" has general application; but in the revelation of August 1, 1831, it was directed to Edward Partridge and his associates in office (D. and C. 58:6a-d). They had been called of God. Knowing this they were to move forward humbly, but with confidence and initiative.

It was the intention of the church leaders that the gathering should be selective rather than general. None were to gather "in haste" or "by flight" (D. and C. 58:12b). Some were not to gather "for many years" (D. and C. 58:9e). Skilled persons "of all kinds" were to be given priority as well as "the rich and the learned, the wise and the noble."

The Saints were admonished to "be subject to the powers that be" (D. and C. 58:5b) as were their neighbors. They were to do this in good spirit and not as though their good intentions gave them a right to be a law to themselves. When they were ill-treated, they were to seek redress within the law (D. and C. 98:10; 102:7; 112:11). To do other than this would have placed them on the same level as their enemies.

Despite the importance of the settlement in Missouri the work of the church as a whole could be more advantageously administered from Kirtland. Joseph and a number of the elders returned, preaching by the way, but they now had a clearer understanding of what was entailed in the Zionic movement.

Questions and Discussion Topics

1. Independence, Missouri, is the "Center Place" for both the Zionic effort of the Saints and the administrative direction of church affairs. What values, do you believe, come from the designation of such a center? limitations?
2. Who were present at the dedication of the place for the temple? Did the church own this place at the time? What was the area of the tract involved? Who purchased this land?
3. What was the work of Bishop Partridge in Independence? Who were his close associates in this work? What instruction was given him regarding his function as a "judge in Israel"?
4. What principle was Sidney Gilbert to observe in his industrial concerns? For what purpose was he to conduct his store? What principles were to guide W. W. Phelps in his business affairs?
5. Why was it important that Oliver Cowdery should be associated with W. W. Phelps in connection with church publications? Why does the church

now sustain the First Presidency as editors in chief of church publications (D. and C. 123:14, Appendix A; 125:11b)?

6. Discuss the significance of the counsel given Bishop Partridge that the Saints should be actively engaged in a good cause. Relate the principle to the encouragement of those who seek to be good stewards.

7. Why is it important that the gathering shall be selective? What priorities should be observed? What varieties of preparation should be made by those who desire to gather or who already live in gathering areas?

8. Not all the laws of the land are wise and just, nor is the administration of these laws always honest and fair. In view of this, what should be the attitude of the Saints toward civil laws and authorities? Note the importance of such principles as love, patience, sacrifice in this connection (I Corinthians 13). How does social action in government, laws, and community standards call for our involvement as agents of change (D. and C. 151:9)?

Exploration 24

SPIRITUAL STANDARDS OF ZION

PREPARATORY READING: *New Commentary*, pages
219-220, 229-230, 236

ADDITIONAL BOOKS NEEDED: Bible, Doctrine
and Covenants

Introduction

Effective Zionic relationships are dependent upon
the spiritual quality of the participants. Careful and
willing observance of the moral law, the realization
and recreation which come from rest and genuine
worship, the power generated in complete dedication
to a great cause, and the strength born of willing
compliance without bargaining are direct
contributions to Zionic effectiveness.

For Consideration

There are many secondary reasons for the
gathering, but the primary ones are spiritual
(D. and C. 58:3b; 59:1a; 140:5c).

Requirements of the moral law had been impressed
on the minds of the Saints at Kirtland (D. and C.
42:6-7). They were reiterated when the pioneers
reached Independence and emphasized again less than
a month later (D. and C. 59:2; 63). They were and are
of the greatest importance.

The expression "a broken heart and a contrite
spirit" occurs repeatedly in the early revelations
(D. and C. 17:7; 19:3; 52:4; 54:1; 55:1; 56:2, 5, 6;

59:2; 94:2). It occurs also in the Psalms and in Isaiah
(Psalms 34:18; 51:17; Isaiah 57:15). It has to do with
awareness of the need for forgiveness and so for
penitence. It is not incompatible with the rejoicing
and the "cheerful hearts and countenances"
mentioned in Doctrine and Covenants 59:3-4.

It is vitally important that the Saints shall reserve
time for worship. A major means to this end is
regular and meaningful Sabbath observance. This
obligation was laid on the Saints from the beginning
(D. and C. 59:2f-h, 3; 68:4; 119:7). Note the
connection between the means of keeping ourselves
"more fully. . . unspotted from the world" and the
counsel of the apostle Paul to the Saints in Rome
(Romans 12:1-2).

A characteristic of Zionic people, wherever we live,
is heartfelt gratitude (D. and C. 59:4-5). Gratitude
needs to be expressed. We should not take for granted
the goodness of God.

Note the relation of fasting and the preparation of
food (D. and C. 59:3, 4). Note, too, the purpose of
fasting as understood in light of this revelation.
Fasting is recommended as a means of grace
(D. and C. 85:21a, 36b; 92:3e; 124:1).

The concern for genuine spirituality is evident
throughout the revelations but should not be so
understood as to decry the importance of education.
Before the journey to Missouri began Oliver Cowdery
(who had been a schoolteacher) was called to select
and write books for school children (D. and C. 55:2a).
Obviously, spiritual quality should direct the use of
education. But there is no salvation in ignorance. Note

that "Moses was learned in all the wisdom of the Egyptians" (Acts 7:22). See also Daniel 1:17.

W. W. Phelps was set apart to be "a printer to the church" (D. and C. 55:2a; 57:5a). Oliver Cowdery was associated with him, but Oliver's major responsibility was apparently "to copy, to correct, and select" what was published (D. and C. 57:5b). Oliver was the "second elder" of the church. Such close association of the leaders of the church with its publishing interests was to become characteristic of church administration (D. and C. 125:11c).

Questions and Discussion Topics

1. "Zionic conditions are no further away nor any closer than the spiritual condition of my people justifies." This is from the revelation of 1947 (D. and C. 140:5c). What does this mean? In what sense was it true in 1831?
2. Discuss, briefly, the importance of the moral law. Discuss its social importance for us.
3. "A broken heart and a contrite spirit" is described in Doctrine and Covenants 59:2e as "a sacrifice unto the Lord thy God in righteousness." What does this mean? Why is it given such prominence? Are there any acceptable substitutes for it?
4. What instruction was given to the Saints in Missouri regarding Sabbath keeping? What later instruction was given to the church in this connection? Why is Sabbath keeping important? How can we meet the spirit of this instruction, yet work on Sunday?
5. Why is it essential that we express our gratitude to

our heavenly Father (D. and C. 59:5b)? What is the relation between gratitude and effective worship? between effective worship and righteousness?

6. What is the essential factor in fasting? How is fasting compatible with the partaking of food? What are the spiritual results of wastefulness? Why is extortion wicked?

7. Why is education important? Under what conditions should it be sought and exercised? What may be its major hazards? strengths? How have we been a movement stressing the growth of intelligence? In what ways have we been anti-education?

8. What is the responsibility of the First Presidency in relation to church publications? In what areas is it limited (e.g., Conference authorizes the inclusion of inspired documents in the Doctrine and Covenants). Why does the church discourage the publication of local spiritual manifestations?

Exploration 25

STEWARDSHIP DEVELOPMENT

PREPARATORY READING: *New Commentary*, **pages 242-244, 251, 260-261, 270-273, 284-286**
ADDITIONAL BOOKS NEEDED: Doctrine and Covenants

Introduction

Effective organization for building the kingdom of God includes recognition of the duties, responsibilities, and rights of those participating, and their dependents. This organization is effective only as the Saints are imbued with the spirit of sacrificial devotion to the Cause.

For Consideration

The law of stewardship was taught among the Saints from the beginning, but the first mention of tithing is in the revelation of September 11, 1831 (D. and C. 64:5). Evidently the principle of tithing applies within the larger principle of stewardship.

The increased membership of the church in Kirtland and in Missouri called for an increase in the number of church authorities and more specific delineation of the responsibilities. The need was most evident with regard to the First Presidency and the Bishopric. The responsibility of the First Presidency in connection with the call or trial of bishops should be noted.

The revelation recorded in Doctrine and Covenants

68 was one of the four received at Hiram, Ohio, early in November 1831 (D. and C. 67, 68, 69, 108). In it the term "First Presidency" was used for the first time (D. and C. 68:2e, 3). The need for such a designation was becoming apparent in order to distinguish between general and local presidencies. Actually, Joseph was not set apart as president of the church and high priesthood until January 25, 1832, and the First Presidency was not fully constituted until March 18, 1833 (D. and C. 80:1b; 87:3).

Those named "stewards over the revelations" were given the right to publish the Book of Commandments. They were not to give the book away but were to live on the proceeds of its publication and consecrate any surplus. This pattern was to be an example for other group stewardships. It was an interesting and necessary modification of the "no purse, no scrip" instruction to traveling missionaries (D. and C. 23:7b, c; 72:3d, 4c; 83:13, 15).

The mood of the early church was that nothing was to hinder the preaching of the gospel. Elders who were willing to do so were instructed to rely for their support on the generosity of those to whom they brought the message. Those having family responsibilities were to rely on neighboring church members. The resources of the general church were very small, but where necessary the elders could draw funds from the bishop (D. and C. 75:4-5). Many of the missionaries actually went on their journeys (e.g., the British mission) after making very scanty provisions for their families.

The principle of the storehouse has its most obvious application in relation to the accumulation of financial and other material reserves. The form taken by the storehouse may change with developing circumstances, but such underlying principles as compassion, sacrifice, and sound judgment are vital to the establishment and regulation of the storehouse contemplated in Doctrine and Covenants 77.

In its larger sense the storehouse principle applies to all the relationships of stewards. Every talent is accompanied by an invitation to share with those who are needy but lack talent, "and this not grudgingly" (D. and C. 70:3d). This calls for goodwill. It also calls for wisdom and sound judgment.

The Saints were told that in temporal things they must be equal (D. and C. 70:3d). This could not be achieved or maintained by mere sharing of goods, for the value of goods depends on who uses them. The Saints sought equality in (a) recognizing that all stewards have primary responsibility for themselves and their own family, (b) seeking to discharge the social responsibilities due to their gifts and situation and (c) consecrating their surplus for the support and welfare of the poor. The endeavor to achieve such equality was a prelude to the achievement of equality "in the bands of heavenly things" (D. and C. 77:1d.

Questions and Discussion Topics
1. Distinguish between the call to tithe and the call to be a steward. Which is the more inclusive? What is the practical meaning of this 'distinction?
2. Where was Bishop Partridge during the later

months of 1831? What development in organization was necessary in Kirtland because Bishop Partridge was not available there? Who was Newell K. Whitney? What was the relation of Elder Whitney to Bishop Partridge? What were the new duties to which Newell Whitney was called?

3. Through whom are calls to the bishopric made known? Why is this important? Why are bishops also high priests?

4. Who were appointed to be stewards over the revelations? Why were the members of this group selected? How were they to be supported?

5. On what principle was the early evangelism of the church financed? In that day this involved many sacrifices, some of which are not now necessary. On what principle is the appointee evangelism of today financed? Would this eliminate the need for sacrifice in order to minister? Why? Why not?

6. What do we mean by "the principle of the storehouse"? What elements are essential to its effective operation? Why?

7. Among other non-material reserves which the church has built and from which the Saints are fed are the history and tradition of the church, our literature, our hymnody, and other worship resources. Discuss the importance of such reserves and the obligation of talented stewards to add to and refine them. Name other similar reserves. What reserve areas could we continue to add?

8. In what ways are the Saints already equal? What further equality should disciples seek? What is the relation between temporal and spiritual equality?

Exploration 26
A SHARED VISION

PREPARATORY READING: *New Commentary*, pages
278-284, Bible, Acts 2:24, 3:15, 4:10, 10:39-41,
13:30-31, 17:31; Romans 10:9; Galatians 1:1
ADDITIONAL BOOKS NEEDED: Doctrine and
Covenants

Introduction

For the Saints of the early Restoration immortality
and eternal life were matters of personal concern.
This is apparent from study of many of the recorded
revelations of which Doctrine and Covenants 76 is
probably the most outstanding.

For Consideration

The record of this vision indicates that it was given
to Joseph Smith and Sidney Rigdon as they
contemplated the meaning of John 5:29. It was no
momentary questioning. They were deeply concerned
over the meaning of the text but unsatisfied. Their
record says that "the Lord touched the eyes of our
understandings." Major conditions of revelation are
human concern, extremity, and need.

Joseph and Sidney were commanded to write while
they were "yet in the Spirit" (D. and C. 76:3k, 4l, 6h).
This was important. The quality of the experience
they were to describe could not be conveyed in words
except as these words served to mediate something
beyond themselves (D. and C. 76:8). Perhaps there is

here a hint of the Spirit in which other scriptures took shape. The initial response of Joseph and Sidney to the vision of God was awe (D. and C. 76:1). This was akin to the experience of Isaiah (Isaiah 6:1-3). Note Doctrine and Covenants 22:1, 7 in this connection. Any adequate report of a vision of God begins on this note.

Deep awareness of the holiness of God always gives rise to a sense of the horror of rebellion against this holiness. It was part of the essential order of creation that after his vision of the matchless holiness of God Isaiah wrote, "Woe is me! For I am undone; because I am a man of unclean lips; for mine eyes have seen the King, the Lord of hosts" (Isaiah 6:5). It was similarly consistent that as part of this vision Joseph and Sidney should be shown the result of the rebellion of Lucifer and of those who joined forces with him (D. and C. 76:3i-4; Isaiah 14:12 ff.).

Belief in the resurrection of Jesus Christ is fundamental to Christianity. Proclamation of the resurrection was at the heart of the ancient apostolic witness. It was altogether fitting that this testimony should be renewed in the Restoration (D. and C. 76:3g).

Although the limitations of time and space make impossible any extending discussion of the celestial, telestial, and terrestrial glories it will be helpful to think on the underlying principles which they proclaim and illustrate. Among these note the following:

(a) Life is here viewed against the background of eternity. In an age in which many live only for the satisfactions of the passing days, this reminder is of the utmost importance.

(b) There is no greater goal for human endeavor than the discovery and fulfillment of the divine purpose in our creation. All other goals are conditioned by our humanity and pertain to this life only.

(c) Creation is still going forward, but we now have part in the process. We ourselves are shaped by the choices we make (D. and C. 28:12). Our God, in wisdom and love, makes the best that can be made from the self we have shaped. The celestial, terrestrial, and telestial glories are all glorious (D. and C. 76:7).

It is to be expected that the more like God persons of the celestial order become, the more likely they are to minister to those of the lower orders (D. and C. 76:7f). This characteristic can be manifested and developed in our present life (D. and C. 16:3c-f, 4).

It is possible to flout so persistently the love which our heavenly Father offers us that we come to disbelieve the offer and even to disbelieve in God. This is more than an intellectual matter. It has to do with the direction and purpose of our lives and the growth of our self-centeredness until we put ourselves in the place of God as though we are the ultimate determiners of our destiny. This is to be in outer darkness.

Questions and Discussion Topics

1. Under what circumstances was the vision of February 18, 1832, given to Joseph Smith and Sidney Rigdon? What did Joseph and Sidney

contribute? How is the credibility of this section enhanced by the fact that it was shared by two persons?

2. What does this section have to say to disciples about the mood in which we should study the scriptures? In what way does the Inspired Version of John 5:29 differ from the King James version?

3. Discuss the meaning of awe. What are its roots? What is the relation between awe and worship?

4. Enumerate reasons why or why not belief in the resurrection is vitally important to Christianity (Romans 1:4).

5. Why were Joseph and Sidney commanded to write while they were "yet in the Spirit" (D. and C. 76:3k, 7w)? Why were they told, later, not to write (D. and C. 76:8a)? Is it required of those who seek understanding today that they shall be "in the Spirit"? Why?

6. What do we mean by the terms "celestial glory, terrestrial glory, and telestial glory"? What qualities in our own lives determine our own "glory"? (See I Corinthians 15:40-41.)

7. How is freedom (the exercise of agency) an essential aspect of celestial glory? Why? May seemingly good men and women fall from realms of glory (D. and C. 2:2b; 17:6d)? Does such a fall take place here as well as in the hereafter (I Corinthians 9:27; 10:12)?

8. Many have died without ever hearing the gospel. About this situation we know very little, but we do know that they are not beyond the love of God. What provision is made for them?

Exploration 27

PRIESTHOOD*

PREPARATORY READING: *New Commentary*, pages 296-305

ADDITIONAL BOOKS NEEDED: Bible, Doctrine and Covenants, *The Priesthood Manual* by Alfred H. Yale

Introduction

Doctrine and Covenants 83 was shown in the early church as "the revelation on priesthood." Its importance is indicated in that it was published as Section 4 of the 1835 edition of Doctrine and Covenants.

For Consideration

It has been the faith of the church that throughout time as the work of God on earth is experienced, its organization has included the ministry of priesthood. The Melchisedic priesthood "continueth in the Church of God in all generations, and is without beginning of days or end of years" (D. and C. 83:2g; see Hebrews 17:3 I.V.). At all times God calls and commissions people to represent him, but they must be called. The emphasis here is on the conviction of the ministers that they have indeed been commissioned of God and on the evidence of their calling demonstrated in the quality of their ministry.

---

*Other aspects of priesthood are discussed in relation to Doctrine and Covenants 42 and 104. Discussion of temples occurs in lesson 28.

Some in the church have affirmed that authority to represent God in the administration of the ordinances of the gospel was gradually lost following the close of the apostolic age. It was sometimes thought that during this period the light of truth was nowhere spread abroad on the earth. This is not sustained by evidence. Many honest and earnest men, women, and children were blessed as they sought to do God's will, even though others in the church had departed from the faith. The Restoration movement was possible only because of the preparation made by reformers, translators, and others of God's people.

Effective administration of the ordinances of the gospel centers in the knowledge of God (D. and C. 83:3). It is therefore related to the entire ministry of the Melchisedic priesthood.

The Aaronic priesthood administers the "preparatory gospel" (D. and C. 83:4c). Their work is of great importance but awaits completion. During the period referred to in Doctrine and Covenants 83:4d the emphasis was on obedience to the law of Moses. But the greater the obedience to the letter of the law, the more clear became the need for obedience to its underlying spirit. (Read Galatians 3:23-24.)

We tend to accept without critical examination things to which we are accustomed or which are affirmed by most of today's society. However, the most important aspects of life belong to an expanded order and are related to the mysteries of the kingdom of God (Matthew 13:11; I Corinthians 2:7; Ephesians 1:15-19; D. and C. 6:3b; 76:2, 3). Quality belief in these enriching ministries depends on the cultivation of the Spirit of God.

Doctrine and Covenants 83, like other revelations, is pervaded by a note of warning. We are counseled to give attention to the seriousness of breaking a covenant made with God (D. and C. 83:6h); of failure to "give *diligent* heed to the words of eternal life" (D. and C. 83:7a); and of treating lightly the gospel message (D. and C. 83:8a, b).

The instruction to the elders that they should give no prior thought to what they should say in their ministry was given to men on the move. The essence of their preaching was to be testimony. But they were to "treasure up in their minds continually the words of life" and they were to relate their message to the situations in which it was delivered—and do so under the guidance of the Spirit.

We are not all able to do all things equally well. But the scriptures indicate that a divinely ordered purpose underlies the diversities of our gifts. The Spirit divides (and has divided) "to every man severally as he will" (I Corinthians 12:11). It is like God to match us for the duties of our day with gifts matured by many generations. In exercising such gifts unique freedom is attained (D. and C. 84:3-4).

Questions and Discussion Topics

1. Why is it important that the movement of divinity shall be evident in the work of the ministry? Consider this in relation to the statement that every member of the priesthood is to be ordained according to the gifts and callings of God

(D. and C. 17:12; 119:8; I Corinthians 2:5).

2. Distinguish between the ordinances and the sacraments of the gospel. (See *The Priesthood Manual* by Alfred H. Yale, page 192, for help.) Which term is more inclusive? What is the relation of the administration of the ordinances to the knowledge of God?

3. What is the major function of the Aaronic priesthood? What do the revelations mean by the term "the preparatory gospel"?

4. In what way does the revelation couple vanity and unbelief? What are the foundations of sound belief?

5. Discuss the instruction to the elders to give no prior thought to what they are to say in their public ministry (D. and C. 83:14d). Under what conditions is this likely to be most effective? Does it always apply? Explain your answer. How does this relate to Section 85:3a, 21b-e?

6. The revelations warn the elders against boasting of mighty works. Compare Doctrine and Covenants 83:11g with 102:7b in this connection.

7. What is the teaching of the revelation concerning lineage and priesthood (D. and C. 68:2; 83:2e; 84:3; 104:8, 18; 130:3, 9; 152:1a)? Does the availability of sons of members of the priesthood give them any right to claim ordination? What other factors apply here?

Exploration 28

TEMPLES

PREPARATORY READING: *New Commentary*, **pages 223-225, 233-234, 296-297, 316-317, 332-334, 337, 370-371**

ADDITIONAL BOOKS NEEDED: Bible, Book of Mormon, Doctrine and Covenants

Introduction

The first mention of the temple in the revelations is where "the spot for the temple" is indicated (D. and C. 57:1d). This may seem abrupt. It should be remembered, however, that the early Saints were keen students of the Bible, with its many temple references, and also the Book of Mormon with its many additional references. Nephi built a temple (II Nephi 4:22-25). Jacob, Mosiah, and Limhi all taught in temples (Jacob 1:17, 2:2, 13; Mosiah 1:27-35, 5:25; Alma 11:22). Christ appeared near the temple in Bountiful. In the thought of the Saints, Zion, the New Jerusalem, and the temple went together (III Nephi 9:58, 10:2, 3; Ether 6:3-10).

For Consideration

The closely related concepts of the gathering and the temple were part of the faith and philosophy of the Restoration from the beginning. In large measure each was dependent on the other. The gathering was to be for mutual aid and for demonstration of the social requirements and values of the gospel. The

122

temple was to be "a place of thanksgiving for all Saints" and of instruction for the ministry (D. and C. 94:3-4).

The promise concerning the building of the temple (D. and C. 83:1-2a, b) led many of the Saints to believe that a temple would be built in Independence in that generation. If this is held to be the intent of the prophecy, it is now clear that it was not fulfilled. In explanation of this some have pointed out correctly that the Saints intended to build a temple but were prevented from doing so for many reasons, e.g., the opposition of their enemies. In this connection reference is made to Doctrine and Covenants 107:15-16 (Appendix A:15-16). The leading elders of the church at that time do not appear to have been unduly troubled by the seeming non-fulfillment of the promise. Further temple blessings were anticipated when the Center Place is redeemed "after many days" (D. and C. 102:10a, b, d).

The Saints of Kirtland were commanded to build a temple. It was to be built as a center of worship and study (D. and C. 85:36-37). The purpose of the temple proposed for the Center Place was set forth from a somewhat different angle the following August. Here the emphasis on the preparation of the ministry is somewhat stronger (D. and C. 94:3-4).

Paraphrasing the late Elder Heman C. Smith (church historian), one notes that much of what was anticipated for the temple in Missouri was fulfilled at Kirtland:

• The Kirtland Temple was built in that generation.

- A cloud which was the glory of the Lord rested upon it and filled the house (D. and C. 83:2).
- The sons of Moses and Aaron offered an acceptable offering (D. and C. 83:6).
- The Kirtland Temple was located on a "consecrated spot" (D. and C. 83:6) the same as the Temple Lot in Independence.
- In dedicating the Kirtland Temple Joseph Smith said that the Lord had commanded the building of the Temple. The only direct command of which we have any record is that in Section 83.
- The Independence Temple was not greatly needed at that time, but the Kirtland Temple was the scene of the great endowment of the ministry ere they were sent out to the nations in a remarkable missionary campaign.

The temples at Independence and Kirtland were intended to be centers of thanksgiving "for all Saints" and "of instruction for all those who are called to the work of the ministry, in all their several callings and offices" (D. and C. 94:3c; 85:39a-b; 149A:6). While any of the Saints could participate in temple services according to their several callings, every effort was to be made to see that only the pure in heart should do so (D. and C. 85:36c, 38, 42; 94:4).

Most of the services of the early church were held in schoolhouses, barns, homes, or outdoors. In none of these places could they duplicate the procedures outlined for temple worship and instruction. Nevertheless the temple ideals did much to shape their less formal gatherings.

Temple functions are more important than any set

form of temple structure. The temple at Kirtland was built for worship and instruction. The temples of tomorrow will look different. They might even consist of central sanctuaries with related buildings which together form a Temple Complex. But the spirit and purpose of temple ministry remain the same. Temples are intended to minister to the fundamental aspects of the life of the church (D. and C. 149:6a).

Lack of any large communities of Saints and also lack of money, combined with doubts as to the divine sanction of ordinances introduced at Nauvoo and other factors, combined to delay temple building by the Reorganization. But interest ran deep as was evident from Doctrine and Covenants 122:6c and from the satisfaction felt when Kirtland Temple came into the possession of the Reorganization. Rich spiritual experiences have been enjoyed at Kirtland since that time, e.g., during the 1950 Conference of High Priests. Although the church has been instructed to prepare to build a temple at the Center Place (D. and C. 149:6), the basic preparation underlying and motivating all other preparations is still dependent on the constantly enriched spiritual quality of the Saints (D. and C. 102:2c, 140:5c).

Questions and Discussion Topics

1. Why did the Saints of the early Restoration accept so readily the command to build temples in Jackson County and at Kirtland?
2. What relationship does temple building have to the gathering?
3. What description was applied to the temple to be

built at Kirtland (D. and C. 85:36b)? Discuss how these temple functions were related to each other.

4. What further temple function was set forth in projecting the temple for Independence? Name some of the promises which at first related to the temple in the Center Place but which were more completely fulfilled at Kirtland.

5. To whom were the temple services available? What limitations were divinely imposed?

6. Suggest ways in which the patterns set for temple worship and instruction might influence soundly the congregational activities of the church.

7. Why is it necessary that the First Presidency be given major responsibility in determining the shape and character of the temple now projected?

8. Summarize the instruction given in 1968 concerning the building of a temple in the Center Place. How is it to be financed (D. and C. 149:6, 149A:5)?

Exploration 29
THE WORD OF WISDOM

PREPARATORY READING: *New Commentary*, **pages 317-319**

ADDITIONAL BOOKS NEEDED: Bible; Church History, Volumes 1, 2; Doctrine and Covenants

Introduction

Obedience to the Word of Wisdom is important. Nevertheless, we are not justified in placing greater emphasis on obedience to the commandments concerning food than on the commandments having to do with other aspects of saintly living. Here, as elsewhere, wisdom and a sense of stewardship must guide.

For Consideration

The Word of Wisdom was given for the benefit of the Council of High Priests assembled in Kirtland and was probably called for by conditions existing then. It should be noted that it was also directed to the church and to "the Saints in Zion." The breadth of its application is indicated, moreover, in that it is said to be "given for a principle, with promise; adapted to the capacity of the weak, and the weakest of all Saints" (D. and C. 86: Introduction).

The revelation was given "in consequence of evils and designs which do and will exist in the hearts of conspiring men" (D. and C. 86:1a). Note the prophetic element here: the revelation anticipated that the evils and designs of conspiring people would persist.

The suggestion that the wine used in the sacrament should be "of your own make" offered a workable procedure in 1833. It is still followed in many congregations, but conditions for producing grape juice have changed in today's society. Commercial juice may be more pure and safe because of government regulations. In other cultures grape juice may be inappropriate while water or coconut juice may be just as symbolic.

The moral obligation to maintain the safeguards essential to protecting our physical stewardship still remains. With many health problems among humankind, the Word of Wisdom has practical application today.

Copies of the Word of Wisdom were sent to the Saints in Missouri "not by commandment or constraint." This was done to avoid, as far as possible, any appearance of dictation from Kirtland. This was necessary because there was already some strain between the two groups. The specific approach was not intended to lessen the importance of the teaching of the Word of Wisdom.

Leaders of the church took seriously the prohibitions of the Word of Wisdom. In 1834 the high council at Kirtland "concurred by vote" in a decision of President Joseph Smith, Jr., that "no official member in this church is worthy to hold an office" if, after being taught these words of wisdom, he neglected "to comply with or obey them" (Church History, Volume 1, page 434). At Far West the congregation voted unanimously not to support stores and shops selling spirituous liquors, tea, coffee, or tobacco (Church History, Volume 2, pages 120 and 140).

There have been times when attempts have been made to make compliance with the Word of Wisdom a test of fellowship in the church. The judgment of the church has been against this. A major reason for reluctance of this kind has been unwillingness to rank compliance with the Word of Wisdom ahead of other tenets of the moral law which may be of even greater social significance. The principle stated by the Lord Jesus concerning tithing seems to have a significant bearing here (Matthew 23:23).

There are many affirmative reasons why wise people avoid addiction to the use of strong drink, tobacco, and deleterious drugs. Among the strongest of these reasons is the fact that such addictions impair the freedom and potential of those addicted.

The story of the Good Samaritan tells of a certain man who "fell among thieves" who beat and robbed him. It then goes on to tell of the Samaritan who had compassion on this man and ministered to him (Luke 10:30-37). But suppose the story was set in today's world and that the "certain man" put himself in the clutches of today's "conspiring men" because he believed their advertising. Would today's story approve the conduct of those who passed by on the other side?

Questions and Discussion Topics

1. Where was the revelation called "the Word of Wisdom" given? To whom was it addressed? To

what wider group was it then addressed? Is any limitation implied concerning the number who should take its counsel seriously? Why was the revelation introduced in such a specific fashion?

2. The cultivation of appetites dangerous to health is part of our society. Which social patterns contribute to the spread of such appetites? Note the effect of the mass media in this connection. What can we do about this?

3. What earlier teachings have the Saints received concerning the use of meat? What additional instruction was now given? Is the use of meat prohibited? What health conditions in 1833 made this wise? How are they different today? same?

4. How do you think that compliance with the provisions of the Word of Wisdom might be advanced acceptably? How can religious aspects of compliance and those recommended by nutritional research be regarded as mutually supporting aspects of a wholistic approach to life?

5. What is the relation of habits to freedom?

6. What connection is there between the Word of Wisdom and other scriptural instruction concerning temperance, adequate sleep, and high moral standards? State the principle involved in terms of our living stewardship as disciples.

7. Why is it important that we should use wholesome food "with prudence and thanksgiving"? What will this require of us? What will it free us to do?

8. The Word of Wisdom warns against habits which "are not good for man." Many honest, kind, and generous persons are the victims of such habits.

These include ourselves, relatives, neighbors, friends. We often regard our addictions as evidences of our freedom and resent "interference" with our freedom of action. Name some things that modern Samaritans may do in this connection, if anything. Name some things that modern Samaritans should not do in this connection. In what respect is the church acting as a wise and good Samaritan? How can your pastoral unit be concerned about any local action of this nature?

Exploration 30

EDUCATION AND THE SCHOOL OF THE PROPHETS

PREPARATORY READING: *New Commentary,* pages 219-220, 313, 315-317, 322-323, 331, 336, Church History, Volume 1, pages 22-23, 524-525, 530, 539, 553, 606

ADDITIONAL BOOKS NEEDED: Doctrine and Covenants

Introduction

Our history and our scriptures combine to indicate the importance of education, but attitude of heart is as important as keenness of mind. The instruction given the early church concerning the School of the Prophets anticipates many of the progressive ideas of today's educators.

For Consideration

The elders of the early Restoration were keenly aware that their essential message was unique and precious (D. and C. 43:4). But they were also sharply aware of lacks which education could offset. There were experienced teachers among them. Schools were among their first concerns wherever they settled.

The importance of preparation, which had been emphasized in early revelations (D. and C. 10:8), was renewed from time to time and was directly related to the spread of the gospel: "I sent you out to testify and warn the people... *therefore*, tarry ye and labor diligently, that you may be perfected in your ministry" (D. and C. 85:22a, 23a).

The importance which the early church placed on education and on common understanding of the principles of the gospel is apparent from the close association of the Presidency with the School of the Prophets and the story of the school conducted by Parley P. Pratt in Missouri. It should be kept in mind that the students were disciples. Their testimony was primary even though their developing skills were of great importance.

Note how the range of study commended to the leading elders and the world vision to which it pointed ran parallel to the world mission of the church (D. and C. 85:20-21; 87:5b; 90:12).

Note, too, the endeavors made to be sure that the ultimate spiritual purpose of the School of the Prophets should be kept to the fore (D. and C. 83:20; 85:36-46; 94).

Despite the unique characteristics of the school in Missouri and Kirtland, the students were to rely on those not of their faith to provide the "best books" they were to study. This ran parallel to their dependence on others for their hymns. Almost all of the teaching was done by church leaders, but there was a notable exception in that the class in Hebrew was taught by a Mr. Seixas.

The "Lectures on Faith" (sometimes called "Lectures on Theology") delivered at Kirtland during the winter of 1834 were prepared for publication in the 1835 edition of the Doctrine and Covenants

(Church History, Volume 1, page 539). They were important in that they set forth the basic theological position of the Saints at that time.

The close association of the School of the Prophets and the temple gave emphasis to the importance of the preparation of the ministry (D. and C. 85:7, 94:3-4). Further emphasis has been given recently (D. and C. 149A:6).

Questions and Discussion Topics

1. What is the relationship of education of the ministry to the spread of the gospel? Is education primary? If not, what is primary? How does this still stress the need for education?
2. When was the first session of the School of the Prophets held? Name some members of the faculty. Who was in general charge of the work of the school? How long did the school continue? What other notable school was held during this period?
3. Discuss the meaning of the injunction given the elders to "seek learning by study and also by faith." How does each influence the other?
4. What were the Lectures on Faith? Where were they given? Where were they published? What is their value? Why?
5. Note the wide range of studies recommended for the School of the Prophets. What does this imply concerning the vision of the early members of the church? How was it related to the success of their world mission?
6. What was the relation of the First Presidency to

the School of the Prophets? Why was this important?
7. To what areas of preparation should today's ministers give unfailing attention? How does today's Temple School meet the needs of the membership in preparation?

Exploration 31

LAW AND ACHIEVEMENT

PREPARATORY READING: *New Commentary*, **pages 308-311, 328-331**

ADDITIONAL BOOKS NEEDED: Bible, Doctrine and Covenants

Introduction

Under the guidance of the Spirit Joseph Smith taught the Saints that in any field of life success is possible only to those who learn and obey the laws operating in that field. This is as true in the spiritual realm as it is on the physical level.

For Consideration

Serious thought concerning the purpose of our creation and that of the world in which we live brings us, before long, to thought of the nature of our Creator. We cannot stop with mere thought of God (Isaiah 55:6-10). We move from thought to wonder and from wonder to worship. This is the mood engendered as we yield ourselves to the spell of the opening paragraphs of Doctrine and Covenants 85.

It is our faith that creation is still going forward and that at every stage it is purposeful. We may be capricious, but the loving purpose of our Creator is unchanging. "His paths are straight and his course is one eternal round" (D. and C. 2:1c). This changeless purpose is built into the structure of the universe (D. and C. 85:3).

It is in the nature of creation that "the spirit and the body is the soul of man" (D. and C. 85:4a). Neither spirit nor body is complete without the other (D. and C. 45:21). Worship, which is of the spirit, finds its completion in service, which is of the body.

"Unto every kingdom is given a law, and unto every law there are certain bounds also and conditions" (D. and C. 85:9b). As best we understand, the laws operating on one level, e.g. mining, are not operative on a different level, e.g. aeronautics. But if there were no law, no built-in and stable nature, there would be chaos. "That which is governed by law is also preserved by law" (D. and C. 85:8a).

Although the laws which are peculiar to any level of existence are not subject to change, they can be used in harmony with laws operating on a higher level. A falling baseball can be kept from the ground by a good catcher. Recognition of the orderly sequence of cause and effect is the basis of modern life.

In a universe whose secrets are hidden but are discoverable by those who learn its laws and operate in harmony with them, there is the steadfastly renewed hope and joy of achievement. On the spiritual level this achievement is called "glory." The level of glory achieved depends on the level of the law obeyed. Fundamental to the highest glory (celestial glory) is life centered in love (Matthew 5:43-44).

The line of progress toward celestial glory proceeds from obedience to what we know is of God (that which is confirmed in us by the spirit of light and truth), by way of worship, repentance, renewal, and still further obedience. Its keynotes are light, truth, and love on higher and higher levels (D. and C. 90:4).

"The glory of God is intelligence. . . light and truth" (D. and C. 90:6a). Intelligence is not just an attribute of God. It "was not created or made" (D. and C. 90:5a). It is our Father's very being, pervading all creative acts. To ignore God is to close one's mind and heart to the light of truth.

Questions and Discussion Topics

1. What contribution does worship make to our understanding of the purpose of creation?
2. Why is it important to remember that "the spirit and the body is the soul of man"? How does the resurrection appear to be related to this definition of soul (D. and C. 85:4b)?
3. Illustrate the fact that "that which is governed by law is also preserved by law."
4. How does the reign of law aid or hamper freedom? Explain your answer.
5. In what sense are carpenters "obedient" to the law built into their materials when they make attractive and useful furniture? Discuss the meaning of obedience in this connection.
6. How may both justice and mercy serve the purpose of God who has created all things according to the law implanted in their being? What is the function of mercy?
7. In what sense is it true that "light and truth forsaketh the evil one"? Why? Illustrate your answer.
8. "The glory of God is intelligence." What does intelligence mean to you in this connection?

Exploration 32
THE PRESIDENCY

PREPARATORY READING: *New Commentary*, **pages 97, 111-114, 131-133, 188-190, 290-291, 320-323; Church History, Volume 1, pages 192-194, 244-247, 282-283**

ADDITIONAL BOOKS NEEDED: Bible, Doctrine and Covenants, Church History, Volume 2

Introduction

"The burden of the care of the church is laid on him who is called to preside over the high priesthood of the church, and on those who are called to be his counselors; and they shall teach according to the spirit of wisdom and understanding, and as they shall be directed by revelation, from time to time."— D. and C. 122:2.

For Consideration

When the church was organized Joseph Smith and Oliver Cowdery were called apostles (D. and C. 17:1, 3; 19:1a). The title had already been applied to Oliver Cowdery and David Whitmer (D. and C. 16:3b). Later it was applied to Joseph and six elders (D. and C. 83:10). The designation appears to have had reference to their witnessing function rather than to an office in the church (D. and C. 19:3b). In these early months witnessing was a major calling of those so named. The work as a whole was directed by Joseph, who was also recognized as a prophet and first elder.

139

With the growth of the church additional organization was needed. The first high priests were ordained at a conference held at Kirtland, June 3 to 6, 1831. The high priesthood is "the Holy Priesthood after the order of the Son of God" (D. and C. 104:1b). To it "all other authorities or offices in the church are appendages" (D. and C. 104:2).

The further official organization of the church continued. Joseph was ordained president of the high priesthood on January 25, 1832. Sidney Rigdon and Frederick G. Williams were called to be counselors to Joseph in revelation received March 18, 1832, and March 8, 1833. These three constituted the quorum of the First Presidency (D. and C. 104:11b). Any further official ordinations would be within the framework now set up; e.g., the twelve are high priests set apart to be "special witnesses of the name of Christ in all the world" (D. and C. 104:11c).

The Saints of the early Restoration paid close attention to biblical precedents. Many were aware of the close association of Aaron and Hur with Moses in the leadership of ancient Israel (Exodus 24:14, 15) and of the eminence of Peter, James, and John in the church of the apostolic age (Acts 12:17, 15:14, 21:18; Galatians 1:19, 2:12). The setting up of a Presidency of three does not appear to have caused any surprise.

The counselors in the First Presidency were "equal" with Joseph in holding "the keys of the kingdom" (D. and C. 87:1-3). This equality had primary reference to the administration of church affairs and the instruction of the ministry (D. and C. 87:3b, c, 5c). However, Joseph and only Joseph was the prophet

(D. and C. 19:1; 43:1, 2).

The revelation of March 28, 1835, says that the Presidency of the Melchisedec priesthood "of necessity" consists of three presiding high priests (D. and C. 104:11a, b). In view of "the burden of the care of the church" (D. and C. 122:2a) and of his own need for intimate understanding and support (D. and C. 6:8), the president is not required to serve alone. Three closely related associates make for stability and strength.

When the church was organized Oliver Cowdery was called to be "second elder," yet when the First Presidency was organized he was not one of those chosen. He was sustained as one of four assistant counselors in September 1837 (Church History, Volume 2, page 107). Even this arrangement was not long continued. We are not sure why these changes in official relations were made. No demotions seem to have been implied. What transpired illustrates the difficulty of fitting capable newcomers into the existing church structure. Oliver's basic calling may possibly have been patriarchal (D. and C. Appendix A:29e).

The Quorum of Twelve was not organized until February 1835. Soon after this the quorum was stated to be "equal in authority and power" to the First Presidency (D. and C. 104:11d). But this equality, like that within the First Presidency itself, was limited. It was most fully and most reasonably expressed in connection with the extension of the work into new fields—e.g., in opening the work in the British Isles. This missionary endeavor was a primary responsibility for the Twelve, but it had to be kept in balance with the total movement of the church (D. and C. 122:1-3; 150:11b) under the First Presidency.

Questions and Discussion Topics

1. Who were the presiding officers of the church during 1830? Why was there no need of a more complex organization for several months? What important office in the church was first filled in February 1831? When were the first high priests ordained?
2. Both before and after the organization of the Quorum of Twelve, leaders of the church were called "apostles." Discuss this in relation to the apostolic calling of the church.
3. When was Joseph Smith ordained president of the high priesthood? By what authority was Joseph so ordained? By what authority have subsequent presidents of the high priesthood been ordained? When was the First Presidency fully organized? Who were counselors in the First Presidency at that time? What was their authority?
4. What is the meaning of the phrase "keys of the kingdom" (D. and C. 26:3; 27:2d; Matthew 16:20 I.V.)? Who were associated with Joseph in holding these keys? Who holds the keys of the kingdom at the present time?
5. What is meant by "the oracles of God" (D. and C. 87:2)? In what sense were the oracles given to the church? How are oracles given today (D. and C. 87:5)?

142

6. What was the immediate task of the First Presidency at this time? What specific studies were recommended to the members of the Presidency? Does such counsel apply to others? How? Why?
7. What are the principles set forth in Doctrine and Covenants 11:4; 120:3a; 122:16b? What is their relationship to the honor attached to official standing in the church?
8. The president of the church, and no other, is called to be "Prophet, Seer, and Revelator" to the church (D. and C. 19:1; 104:42b). We are also told that prophecy is one of the gifts of the Holy Spirit shared by members of the body of the church (D. and C. 46:7d). How are these consistent with each other? different? In what way does the designation of the school presided over by the First Presidency as "the School of the Prophets" have significance here? How is Section 149:6a consistent with this designation?

Exploration 33
EXPULSION AND REDRESS

PREPARATORY READING: *New Commentary*, pages
338-349; Church History, Volume 1, pages 289-291,
303-367, 379-388

ADDITIONAL BOOKS NEEDED: Bible, Doctrine
and Covenants

Introduction

From the beginning of the settlement in Missouri
there was friction between the Saints and their
"Gentile" neighbors. This culminated in the expulsion
of the Saints from Jackson County and, later, from
Missouri. It was against a general background of
some of these events that Joseph received the
revelations now to be discussed.

For Consideration

It was the expectation of the Saints who pioneered
the gathering to Missouri that, under the guidance of
the Almighty, they would build Zion as a city of
refuge and a place of safety for the Saints (D. and C.
45:12c-d). They were bitterly disappointed. Some of
the reasons for their expulsion from Jackson County
and, later, from the state, were related to the times.
Other reasons were more fundamental and must be
considered for any future Zionic enterprises.

The most obvious reason given for the expulsion of
the Saints is that many of the people of frontier
Missouri were selfish and cruel. These attitudes can be

documented among some "gentiles" and Saints. But not all were like that. Some were leaders of the communities where they lived. Some of these were religious leaders fanatically predisposed to fight persons of different faiths. But, again, not all ministers were like that. And it may be noted that some Saints were predisposed to an overemphasis on being the "chosen people." The principle of Zionic gathering requires that those who gather recognize the rights of surrounding "Gentiles" and do so with understanding and generosity. These factors are permanent. They should inform and guide the Saints in their relations with each other and with those not of our faith.

Of possibly greater importance were the factors making for division among the Saints themselves. These were both individual and social. The revelation of December 1833 says that "there were jarrings and contentions, and envyings and strifes, and lustful and covetous desires among them; therefore by these things they polluted their inheritances" (D. and C. 98:3a). Such people could not stand the strains and sacrifices involved in kingdom building (D. and C. 85:20); nor, it appears, can we (D. and C. 140:5c).

Many of those who had come to Missouri were "truly humble" and were "seeking diligently to learn wisdom and to find truth" (D. and C. 94:1a, f). But these suffered with those of their number who were less worthy than they. Life is a community enterprise. This is particularly true of life in the kingdom.

People show their quality in crisis. Remember that after the printing plant of the *Star* was destroyed the mob tarred and feathered Edward Partridge and

145

Charles Allen. Three days later, Edward Partridge, John Covill, John Whitmer, W. W. Phelps, A. S. Gilbert, and Isaac Morley, leaders among the Saints, offered themselves as ransom for the church. They were willing to be scourged or die if that would appease the anger of the mob (Church History, Volume 1, pages 316, 350-353). Remember, too, the faith and courage of the unknown Saints who were involved in these outrages but also remained true to their convictions.

In the midst of this persecution the Saints were instructed to support and proceed according to the law of the land in seeking redress (D. and C. 95:2). This was not mere theorizing. Obedience required stringent self-discipline. They were to accept such injustices as could not be overcome in their situation. But they were also to seek diligently for honest, wise, and good men who could be supported in places of political responsibility (D. and C. 95:2d).

The counsel given did not require those persecuted to submit without protest. They were justified in defending themselves against repeated aggression. But they were not to hold resentment nor seek revenge. As a basic principle they were to "renounce war and proclaim peace" (D. and C. 95:3d, 5-7).

God's living kingdom is built according to the principle of sacrifice and difficulty. Yet more important sacrifices are required of the builders. Jesus taught this in the Sermon on the Mount (Matthew 16:24). He illustrated it on Calvary. He has reminded us of this in our own time (D. and C. 64:5a; 130:7d; 147:5b). These sacrifices are preludes to "a far more

146

exceeding and eternal weight of glory" (II Corinthians 4:17; Hebrews 12:2; D. and C. 95:3b-d).

Questions and Discussion Topics

1. Name some reasons why the earlier settlers in Missouri persecuted the Saints. What may we learn from considering these reasons? Has such consideration any value for today?

2. What valuable property was destroyed by the mob July 20, 1833? What church members were especially mistreated? Name the leaders of the church who should be remembered for their heroism in this situation.

3. Why were the instructions now received regarding the civil law particularly timely? What is the significance of the phrase, "When the wicked rule the people mourn"? What political activity is rightfully expected of the Saints in addition to supporting the Constitution and laws in harmony therewith?

4. Is this counsel referred to in Question 3 practicable in our personal concerns today? in economic affairs? in national affairs?

5. The Saints had been warned against contention (D. and C. 3:15c-d), lust (D. and C. 42:7, 46:4, 63:5), covetousness (D. and C. 18:3, 85:38). Knowing this, they had traveled to Missouri at considerable sacrifice. Now these are named as factors in their expulsion from their land of promise. It has been suggested that there is a time element between recognizing an attitude or an act to be sinful and overcoming it. In what way is this

so? What salvation is there in renouncing sin even though it has not yet been fully overcome?

6. Outline the instruction on self-restraint and forgiveness in Doctrine and Covenants 95:5-7. Discuss the application of this procedure in modern life.

7. What should be the Latter Day Saint attitude toward participation in the duties of citizenship? toward the promotion of industrial peace? toward the promotion of international peace?

8. How is self-preservation the first law of nature for parents? Is it the first law of nature for any good man or woman? What claim do persons have for divine protection or vindication when they take the law into their own hands? Can people effectively practice the law of forgiveness unless there is in their hearts something of the love of God for their neighbor? Explain.

Exploration 34

ZION SHALL NOT BE MOVED

PREPARATORY READING: *New Commentary*, pages
336-338, 348-354, 357-361, 366-371; Church
History, Volume 1, 439-442, 447, 451-452,
454-457; Doctrine and Covenants 83:2; 94:1-5;
97:4a; 98; 100:1-6

ADDITIONAL BOOKS NEEDED: Bible

Introduction

The spiritual experiences of the early Saints and the
prophetic leadership of Joseph Smith, Jr., combined to
convince them that it is divine intention to build the
kingdom of God on earth in this "dispensation of the
fullness of times." When the location of the Center
Place was indicated the pioneers went there in faith
and at great cost. When they were expelled from their
first place of settlement it was inevitable that they
should reexamine their faith in light of what had
happened to them. It was then that Joseph wrote,
addressing himself to the crucial fact of the situation,
"Zion can not fall, neither be moved out of her place,
for God is there, and the hand of the Lord is there"
(D. and C. 94:5b).

For Consideration

The heartening word was not, "Zion will not fall."
It was much stronger than this. It was, "Zion cannot
fall." This is because the Zionic enterprise is born of
the very nature of God. Those who are good and wise

149

have been challenged by the hope of the kingdom all down the ages. But it cannot be built by men and women alone. Essentially it is possible because of God.

The promise made to the Saints in the name of God pushed back the horizons of their faith. It bade them look beyond their present trials to their more fundamental certainties. Moreover, it sounded familiar. It was akin to the reassurance brought by the Old Testament prophets (Isaiah 35:10, Jeremiah 31:16), and its phrasing reminded them of the words of Jacob in II Nephi 5:90-99. They found comfort in the promises of God down the ages.

With the promise that they would return in a literal, physical sense, came renewed emphasis on what would make this return significant. They were told that "this is Zion, the pure in heart" (D. and C. 94:5c). This was not new (D. and C. 34:5b), but its emphasis during a period of persecution was of great importance. It affirmed that what happens to disciples is not ultimately important, but what happens within them and among them. Consider what illumination this brought to the "truly humble" pioneers who were "seeking diligently to learn wisdom and to find truth" (D. and C. 94:1, 2f; John 10:28-29; Hebrews 11:6).

It was necessary that such comfort and reassurance as was contained in the revelations of August 2 and 6, 1833, be sent to the Saints in Missouri at that time, even though full details of their expulsion from Jackson County were not yet available. Four months later the promise that "Zion shall not be moved out of her place" was renewed, and this clearly referred to a

150

regathering in Missouri (D. and C. 98:4e-h). Moreover, the terms of the regathering were also renewed (D. and C. 98:5i, j).

The endeavor to gather was to continue (D. and C. 98:9a, d). To this end the call was sent to the eastern churches to contribute funds with which to purchase land in Missouri (D. and C. 98:9f). It was in this sense that the land was to be "redeemed" (D. and C. 98:10c). Careful preparations were made and some money, food, and clothing were accumulated, but there were not enough resources in hand by the time the needs of the Missouri Saints required that the relief expedition set out. The company that went to Missouri, known as "Zion's Camp," distributed the supplies they had brought. They found that their resources were inadequate to fulfill their entire purpose. Zion's Camp disbanded soon after reaching Missouri. No one knows what might have happened had more support been given to the members of the camp. It is clear, nonetheless, that the kingdom enterprise must involve the willing cooperation of many men and women of faith (D. and C. 102:8a, 9a).

Some of the members of Zion's Camp stayed in "the regions round about." These were advised to "carefully gather together, as much in one region as can be consistently with the feelings of the people" and here they were to pursue their spiritual purpose while taking care not to repeat the boasting which had irritated the people of Jackson County (D. and C. 102:6-7b-c). The distinctive values of the gospel and the gathering were to be demonstrated in the way of life of the disciples rather than in recital of their expectations.

An unexpected but vitally important result of the expedition of Zion's Camp was that in February 1835 the charter members of the Quorum of Twelve and a number of the first members of the Seventy were chosen from among those who had been part of this company (Church History, Volume 1:540-550). These men had proved themselves and were welcomed to places of leadership.

The Saints had been warned not to gather in haste, but to have all things prepared before them (D. and C. 102:3c-f), and as a result of their experiences they saw the range of this preparation become broader. Any such gathering as was now contemplated called for social as well as individual preparation, the accumulation of many divers resources, and such wise and humble concern in things of the spirit as would make possible the further endowment of the Holy Spirit.

Questions and Discussion Topics

1. In what respect is it true that "Zion cannot fall, neither be moved out of her place"?
2. What do you think will be the characteristics of a community of the pure in heart? Think in terms of integrity, cooperation, purposiveness, freedom, and peace.
3. If we accept with faith and gratitude the description of Zion as "the pure in heart" what will this require of us in respect to the primary

areas of kingdom building? unity with our brothers and sisters in fellowship and service? enriching our worship life?

4. Name factors in the failure of the initial attempt to gather which are apparent to us but which were not so apparent to the pioneers at that time. Comment on the importance of these factors for us today.

5. The early Saints were told that in gathering it was important to "let all things be prepared before you" (D. and C. 98:9). Discuss whether this is suitable counsel for all Saints, wherever they live and whether or not they expect to gather. Is it reasonable to consider congregations of the Saints as preliminary gathering centers? Why? Why not?

6. What was the purpose of Zion's Camp? Why did it fall short of success? In what respect was it of great importance in the development of the organization of the church? Why?

7. Discuss the meaning of such statements as these: "The redemption [of Zion] must needs come by power" (D. and C. 100:3e); "All victory and glory is brought to pass unto you through your diligence, faithfulness, and prayers of faith" (D. and C. 100:7a); "Zion can not be built up unless it is by the principles of the law of the celestial kingdom" (D. and C. 102:2c).

8. What was the influence of the regathering to Independence and the regions round about in the life and ministry of the church? What functions does the Center Place have in the life of the church?

Exploration 35
HIGH COUNCILS

PREPARATORY READING: *New Commentary*, pages
186-187, 354-357; Church History, Volume 1,
pages 429-433, 503-505, 515, 523, 531-532;
Doctrine and Covenants 42:22; 99; 104:14-15;
122:6; 129:7

Introduction

High councils have both original and appellate*
jurisdiction as trial courts. However, with the growth
of the number of bishops, local bishops courts can
often serve to better advantage. The advisory function
of high councils is of steadily growing importance in
bringing a wide variety of experience and judgment to
bear on the problems of church growth and
administration.

For Consideration

Doctrine and Covenants 99 is not in the usual form
in which records of revelatory experience have been
received and approved by the church. It should be
noted that when the minutes of the organization of
the council were approved this was with the
understanding that "if the president should hereafter
discover any lack in the same he should be privileged
to fill it up" (Church History, Volume 1, page 432).
In President Smith's report of his organization of the

---

*Power to review decisions.

High Council of Zion he stated that he did so "agreeably to the revelation given at Kirtland" and then "read the revelation on the subject" (Church History, Volume 1, page 503).

The High Council of Zion was organized by President Joseph Smith on July 3, 1834. This was a local organization with David Whitmer, W. W. Phelps, and John Whitmer as presidents (Church History, Volume 1, page 503). The organization at Kirtland was considered "the high council of the seat of the First Presidency of the church" (D. and C. 99:11, 14; also note D. and C. 122:12) and had church-wide as well as local jurisdiction.

For a time the high council was the most important of the councils of the church and advised the Presidency on matters which afterwards came to be considered within the province of other quorums and councils. Joseph Smith said while in Missouri, but apparently in relation to the general council, that if he should be taken away "the will of the Lord might be known [through this council] on all important occasions in the building up of Zion and establishing truth in the earth" (Church History, Volume 1, page 503).

Four high councils are mentioned in the Doctrine and Covenants. They are the "Standing High Council" consisting of twelve high priests presided over by any one of the members of the First Presidency (D. and C. 104:15); the "Traveling High Council" consisting of twelve apostles presided over by one of their number (D. and C. 104:13, 16); the "stake high councils" consisting of twelve high priests presided over by a member or members of the stake presidency (D. and C. 104:14); and "high councils abroad" which are called in emergencies and consist of twelve high priests presided over by one of their number (D. and C. 99:11, 12).

The World Church Standing High Council and, within the area of their responsibility, the stake high councils are courts of original jurisdiction in such matters as the trial of high priests (D. and C. 68:3; 104:34, 37; 122:10a-b; 126:11). The ordination of high priests must be approved by a World Conference or a high council (D. and C. 17:17; 120:2d).

High councils have advisory functions to the Presidency and the Bishopric. They advise, on request, concerning such matters as ministry to the poor (D. and C. 42:10; 122:6c-e), the management of the properties of the church (D. and C. 122:5d-e, 6f), the gathering (D. and C. 122:6f). In the fairly recent past the advice of the standing high council has been sought concerning the building of the Auditorium, the rehabilitation of church finances, and the purchase and sale of church properties.

While high councils have important functions in the World Church and in stakes it should be kept in mind that these functions are advisory. In themselves high councils have no right of initiation. The administrative authorities, spiritual and temporal, may ask the advice of the appropriate councils but administrative action is always taken on the authority of the administrative officers concerned.

Questions and Discussion Topics

1. What is the first step in dealing with cases of

difficulty within the church (D. and C. 42:23)? Who should take the initiative toward settlement? At what point should members of the priesthood be brought into the endeavors toward reconciliation?

2. What courts are provided for in the church law? Which of these are temporary and which are permanent? What church official is described as a "judge in Israel"?

3. Enumerate the types of high councils contemplated in the law. What is the function of each? Who presides over each?

4. When was the Standing High Council of the church first organized? How had the work of the council been done prior to that time?

5. How are members of high councils appointed? How are emergency members of the council selected?

6. Who may preside over the Standing High Council? What resource does he have in situations where the law is not adequate or not clearly understood?

7. What do we mean when we describe a high council as a "court of original jurisdiction"? as an appellate court? In what matters is the decision of the high council final? What makes this so?

8. How do high councils seek to safeguard the rights of those accused in court actions? How is the accused represented? Who initiates decisions in judicial matters in the high council? What is then needed to complete action?

Exploration 36

THE ORDERS OF PRIESTHOOD

PREPARATORY READING: *New Commentary*, pages
90-94, 296-304, 371; Doctrine and Covenants
16; 103; 104:1-10, 17, 30:31d, 38-41

ADDITIONAL BOOKS NEEDED: Church History,
Volume 2

Introduction

Some of the ministries that the church must offer in
both organized areas and in new fields were
anticipated by the revelation concerning the call of
the Twelve. This had been given before the church
was organized (D. and C. 16) and the instruction was
augmented in subsequent revelations (D. and C. 17,
42, 68, 83, 84; note Explorations 10 and 27).

For Consideration

The world mission of the church was in the minds
and hearts of the leading elders from the beginning.
What this meant did not become clear as to principles
and procedure except as the problems of church
expansion confronted them.

The success of the missionaries gave rise to the need
for pastors who could care for the new converts and
build them into stable groups. While all were called
to bear testimony of the Restoration, not all were
equally skilled in testimony and pastoral care. There
was need for both proclaiming and nurturing
ministries.

158

The transition characteristic of this period is illustrated in the revelation to Warren A. Cowdery. In it he was called to serve as a *presiding* high priest but given duties largely akin to those of a seventy except that he was to minister in areas near to his home (D. and C. 103:1a). This was in November 1834. The principles underlying the instruction previously given concerning the various callings within the priesthood were now set forth more clearly. All ministerial callings belong to one of two types. They are of the Melchisedec Order and have to do with administration on a spiritual level (D. and C. 104:3, 7, 9), or they are of the Aaronic Order which is an "appendage" to the Melchisedec priesthood (D. and C. 104:8b) and administer in "outward ordinances—the letter of the gospel" (D. and C. 104:10). The concern of members of the Aaronic priesthood is with "the preparatory gospel, which is a gospel of repentance and of baptism, and the remission of sins, and the law of carnal commandments" (D. and C. 83:4c).

The graduated functions of the various offices of the priesthood arise out of the necessities of spiritual organization. Men are not ordained as a special favor to them but according to their gifts and callings and as a means of service in the church. Strictly speaking there is no promotion or demotion in the priesthood. Some quorums carry with them a wider range of administrative authority and responsibility than others do, but this wider range of authority arises out of necessity and is not bestowed as a special honor.

The revelation of March 1835 called for the ordination of evangelical ministers in all large branches of the church (D. and C. 104:17). This priesthood was intended "to be handed down from father to son" (D. and C. 104:18), and in this it was like the lineal descent planned for the bishopric (D. and C. 68:2; 83:3a; 104:32). High priests can officiate in any office in the priesthood when occasion requires (D. and C. 68:2d; 104:5). Many high priests serve as bishops under this rule and high priests have also been ordained to serve as patriarch-evangelists.

The revelation envisioned the building of large branches or clusters of small branches in sufficiently close proximity to each other to make feasible the organization of quorums. The quorums of elders may have up to forty-eight members, teachers up to twenty-four members, and deacons up to twelve members (D. and C. 104:38-41). The calling of the presidents of the various quorums is to "sit in council with the members of their quorums," "to teach them their duty," and they are to do this "according to the covenants." In the Reorganization local quorums have functioned most successfully in stakes. The emphasis is in sharing experience in their several ministries, thus maintaining a growing body of understanding within the quorums down the years.

It was evident that if the apostles were to be eagerly concerned to push the work into new fields, they must leave the local ministry in the care of those called to this work. Yet it appears that they must maintain sufficiently close contact with large branches and smaller but contiguous branches to designate evangelical ministers to serve there. It proved difficult to know where to draw the lines, but probably the best example of how the Twelve functioned was in the British mission (Church History, Volume 2, pages 484-497).

Questions and Discussion Topics

1. What are the two major divisions of priesthood? Why is the Melchisedec priesthood so called? What title may be applied to all members of the Melchisedec priesthood? What offices are included in the Melchisedec priesthood?

2. What is meant by such statements as "The Melchisedec priesthood holds the right of presidency" (D. and C. 104:3b), "[the] Melchisedec priesthood is to hold the keys of all the spiritual blessings of the church" (D. and C. 104:9a), and "agreeably to the covenants and commandments of the church" (D. and C. 104:7)?

3. What orders of the priesthood are said to be "appendages to the Melchisedec priesthood" (D. and C. 83:5; 104:2, 8)? What does this mean?

4. Why is the Aaronic priesthood so called? What are the offices in this priesthood? Who presides over the Aaronic priesthood? Is this an administrative or an educational presidency? What is the relation between the Aaronic and the Levitical priesthood?

5. Why is the Aaronic priesthood called "the lesser priesthood"? What is the meaning of these terms which are applied to members of the Aaronic priesthood: "The preparatory gospel," "the law of carnal commandments" (D. and C. 83:4c), or "outward ordinances—the letter of the gospel" (D. and C. 104:10)?

6. In what offices may high priests function? Under whose direction do they serve? Who may serve in their stead when high priests are not available? In what offices do high priests serve when those having a prior lineal calling are not available?
7. Through whom are evangelists called to serve in this office? What priesthood do evangelists hold? Where do they serve? What are their qualifications (D. and C. 137:4b-c)?
8. What is the function of quorums? What numerical limits are set for various quorums? Where do quorums tend to function most effectively? Why? Relate the "tradition of the elders" to the effective functioning of the quorums of the priesthood.

Exploration 37
THE PRESIDING QUORUMS

PREPARATORY READING: *New Commentary*, **pages 372-374, 377-381, 383-385; Church History, Volume 1, pages 537-559; Doctrine and Covenants 104, 105**

Introduction

As the church grew, the officers needed to direct its witnessing and stabilizing functions were called, and their duties in relation to the church at that stage were outlined. Further growth called for further refinement of the administrative structure. Secondary responsibilities were then relinquished and became the primary responsibilities of new quorums and councils. The standing high council, for example, gave place to the Twelve in directing missionary expansion. The transition was not always smooth, but the necessity for it was apparent. The 1835 revelation directed to the Twelve was of major importance in this connection.

For Consideration

It was imperative that the center of authority should be made clear, and the revelation to the Twelve did this. Joseph Smith presided as president of the high priesthood (D. and C. 104:31e). In this presidency two others were associated with him to form a presiding quorum (D. and C. 104:11b). The prophetic function of Joseph was unique in that he

163

was "a seer, a revelator, a translator, and a prophet; having all the gifts of God which he bestows upon the head of the church" (D. and C. 104:42b). In the presiding functions of the First Presidency the counselors were "accounted as equals" with Joseph (D. and C. 87:3a).

The instruction to "the Twelve Apostles, or special witnesses of the name of Christ in all the world" (D. and C. 104:11c-d) was directed to them as a quorum. Their first mission was conducted as a quorum (Church History, Volume 1, pages 562-566) as were others (Church History, Volume 2, page 495). They served under the direction of the First Presidency in building up and regulating all the affairs of the church (D. and C. 104:12; 122:3b).

The quorums of seventies were organized late in February 1835. This office had not been mentioned in the revelations prior to this time. The Seventy were now designated as special witnesses who were to serve under the Twelve and share with them the responsibility of carrying the word into all the world (D. and C. 104:11e, 14, 16, 43). In this their calling is distinct from that of other members of the priesthood.

The organization of the Twelve and Seventy put evangelism on a more regularly organized basis. They were *the* missionary quorums. Although high priests and elders and others continued to bear testimony as before, the Twelve now began to assign missions and to make planned efforts to build stable church units in such places as the eastern states and in Great Britain (D. and C. 105:2b, 8a).

The revelation provided that the Presidency,

164

Twelve, and Seventy were to be "equal in authority and power" (D. and C. 104:11d, e), but decisions must be unanimous after free discussion and must be arrived at "in holiness" (D. and C. 104:11f-i). There were obviously some limitations on this equality, for the Twelve did not share all responsibilities of the Presidency nor did the Seventy share all those of the Twelve. But the sense of equality brought some clear advantages. Both the Twelve and the Seventy were encouraged by the Presidency to consider their specific functions in terms of the total well-being of the church, for they belonged to general quorums. Then, too, when the Twelve were far from Kirtland (as when they were in England) and were required to make decisions in unfamiliar situations, they could act with authority after their free quorum discussions.

The Presidency, who are apostles and high priests, preside over all the work of the church in all the world. But this Presidency is exercised with and through the high priests. These carry great responsibilities in their several assignments, so that much of the work of the Presidency in relation to them is concerned with integrating their ministry with that of others to the end that unity, balance, and power are achieved.

As long as the members of the Presidency and the local high priests were available in stake areas, the demands of the work in new fields required the Twelve to give their major attention to these fields (D. and C. 105:6-7). They were not to be unduly concerned, for example, with affairs at Kirtland (D. and C. 105:11a); but as the Twelve entered more and more fully into their work of ordaining and setting in order all the other offices of the church (D. and C. 104:30) their close kinship with the Presidency became more and more apparent. They constituted the only high priestly quorum having church-wide administrative responsibilities, after the First Presidency, and after a time, it was only natural that they be recognized as "next in authority in spiritual things" (D. and C. 122:5b).

The instruction concerning the duties of the Twelve which was embodied in Doctrine and Covenants 104 was augmented in consultation between the Presidency and Twelve. It was summed up by President Smith and approved by the council (Church History, Volume 1, page 549). Its meaning and ramifications became clear as the Twelve pushed out in their work. That the organic structure of the church, now completed, should have proved so fully adequate to the demands of our history is a major evidence of the divine direction prompting it.

Questions and Discussion Topics

1. What are the distinctive duties of the president of the church? What presiding responsibilities does he share with his counselors (D. and C. 122:2)?
2. Note the functions of the president of the church as set forth in Doctrine and Covenants 43:1-2. Are these functions shared by any other member of the priesthood (D. and C. 27:2)? Why is this necessary?
3. In what manner do the members of the high priesthood, and especially those of the First Presidency, depend on the support of the members

of the church (D. and C. 17:16a; 43:3e; 104:11b; 118:3-4; 120:2a; 124:5b)?

4. What are the primary duties of the twelve apostles? Under whose direction do they serve? Why is the Quorum of Twelve called "a traveling presiding high council" (D. and C. 104:12)?

5. What are the duties of the Seventy? Under whose direction do they serve? In what regard do their duties differ from those of the elders? For how many quorums of Seventy does the law provide?

6. In what sense are the Presidency, Twelve, and Seventy "equal"? What are the conditions of this equality? What do we mean when we call the members of these quorums "general authorities of the church" (D. and C. 99:13)? What responsibility does this calling place on the general authorities? Are there any other general authorities? Who are they?

7. Why is the president of the church said to be "the presiding high priest over the high priesthood of the church" (D. and C. 104:31e)? Are any high priests excluded from this presiding responsibility? Through what groups of high priests is the presidency of the high priesthood expressed?

8. How is the high priesthood described in the Doctrine and Covenants? What are the characteristics of truly high priestly ministry? In what offices may high priests serve?

Exploration 38
GROUP STEWARDSHIPS

PREPARATORY READING: *New Commentary*, **pages 284-287, 292-293, 363-366; Doctrine and Covenants 70, 77, 81, 93, 101**

Introduction

All the Saints knew themselves to be called to be stewards. Some of the leaders had been instructed to form group stewardships to manage church enterprises in Kirtland and Independence (D. and C. 70:1; 72:4). It was highly desirable that these affairs (publishing, etc.), which were of importance to the entire church, be promoted by church leaders. However, the loss of the properties of the church and of the Saints in Jackson County made it impossible to continue this arrangement. The United Order was accordingly dissolved.

For Consideration

The dissolution of the United Order was agreed upon at a council held in Kirtland in April 1834, before the relief expedition left for Missouri. This action was dictated by the evident facts of the Missouri situation. Those responsible apparently were reluctant to proceed without further inspired direction; the revelation of April 1834 confirmed what had been agreed, probably including the assignment of the properties of the Order to individual stewards. This is one of the many points at which further background information would be an aid toward better understanding. We might be better informed, particularly concerning the freedom of decision apparently exercised in council and the reason for succeeding revelation.

One of the major stewardships in Jackson County was that of the bishop and his associates who had been charged with the allocation of inheritances, the receipt of surplus, the management of the storehouse, and the care of the poor. This was of the essence of his calling, which was shared by the bishop of Kirtland. Both of them continued to exercise this calling despite changing circumstances, as have their successors to this day.

While the dissolution of the Order was undoubtedly related to events in Missouri (D. and C. 100:1; 101:9c) the revelation relates it to the breaking of the covenant by members of the Order through covetousness (D. and C. 101:1c, 9d). Covetousness is a basic and continuing problem (D. and C. 18:3b).

Although the United Order was dissolved, the principle of stewardship continued. The basic concern was again set forth: the practice of brotherhood in promoting and maintaining equality of opportunity according to needs and capacities.

Publication of "the fullness of my scriptures and the revelations" (D. and C. 101:10c) continued to be important and was made the responsibility of the "stewards over mine [the Lord's] house" (D. and C. 101:10c). These were evidently the "stewards over the revelations and commandments" (D. and C. 70:1) who were available in Kirtland. For this work a distinctive treasury was to be organized (D. and C. 101:11a). The "stewards over the revelation" had other stewardship responsibilities in addition to those involved at this point.

Other properties in and around Kirtland were to be managed by the newly organized "United Order of the Stake of Zion" (D. and C. 101:9a, 12). This was an organization for mutual aid and the care of the poor through the consecration of surplus.

The organization and maintenance of the United Order were conditioned, to a substantial degree, by the interlocking of the religious, social, and economic situations in Kirtland and Independence. With changed circumstances joint endeavors of vital importance to the church have tended more and more to become the concern of general officers and their associates—publishing; farm management; care of the aged, the sick, and the poor.

The group enterprise in Kirtland was severely handicapped and at times was unsuccessful. The chief reason appears to have been that in a religiously motivated community it was taken for granted that credit must be liberal. When the high expectations of the borrowers did not materialize neither they nor their creditors had adequate resources.

The principle involved in relation to the United Order was stewardship. The method used was joint ownership and administration by a representative group. Note that both the principle and the need for joint action remained. The method could be adjusted, as was done in harmony with Doctrine and Covenants 101, but the principle must be maintained and the problem must be again approached in the light of the changed situation.

Questions and Discussion Topics

1. Relate, briefly, the prior history of the United Order of Enoch. Why was it now necessary to dissolve this Order?

2. What do you think were some of the effects in Missouri of the dissolution of the United Order? Comment on the importance of commitment to the basic tasks of the church in terms of constructive response to local disappointments.

3. What was the high value placed on the publication of the scriptures by early leaders as indicated in Doctrine and Covenants 101:10c, d, 11? What significance does the message in Doctrine and Covenants 83:8 have in light of our frequent failure to study the scriptures?

4. Throughout church history many Saints have functioned as stewards within group stewardships. Consider the concept of group stewardship with the stewardship of church membership, priesthood, and parenthood. Note other such examples of group stewardships.

5. How are the institutions of the church group stewardships? In what ways are they opportunities for exercising individual stewardships?

6. Stewardships may be exercised as members of groups whose other members may not be stewards, e.g. employers, employees, teachers, students. Discuss this statement in terms of an effective Zionic testimony by the Saints.

7. Keeping in mind the credit problems experienced by the Kirtland group stewardship enterprises, what suggestions have you for consideration in the development of group stewardships in industry and government?

Exploration 39

MARRIAGE AND CIVIL GOVERNMENT

PREPARATORY READING: *New Commentary,* **pages 204-205, 339-340, 397-399; Doctrine and Covenants 49:3a; 95:2; 111, 112**

Introduction

The sections of the Doctrine and Covenants on marriage (111) and governments and laws in general (112) are not revelations. However, they embody principles derived from study of the revelations, have been accepted in the church throughout our history, and have been included in the text of the Doctrine and Covenants rather than being designated as "appendices" by action of the World Conference as was done with other sections in 1970.

For Consideration

Stable marriages and sound family life are built on prior consideration of significant priorities. These priorities are obviously personal and social. The church affirms that they are also spiritual. "Marriage is ordained of God unto man" (D. and C. 49:3a).

One of the foundations of sound Christian marriage is the maturity of the contracting parties. It is not possible to enter meaningfully into a relation which promises sustained mutual companionship between growing persons unless the contract is based on mature and elevated consideration of the nature of marriage. This maturity is not primarily a matter of

173

age but rather of the wisdom and courage required to consider values and the costs and consequences of divergent ways of life.

Christian marriage has its unique inclusiveness and exclusiveness. Each is vital to the other. They have not so much to do with sexual conduct as they do with such mutual fulfillment as can be reached only in a partnership of love and sacrificial devotion.

Christian marriage is intended to be mutually life-fulfilling. It is a way of life whose necessary disciplines and sacrifices are challenged by many forces in today's society. Marriage needs increasing faith, courage, and forbearance.

One of the vital elements in Christian marriage is the mutual love of husband and wife. This is much more than a superficial physical, intellectual, or emotional attraction. At its best it involves acting lovingly toward each other in all manner of situations. In this it is akin to the love manifest in the life of Jesus. Marriage is empowered and sustained by the love of God. Here it finds its sources of nobility, hope, and endurance.

It is in view of such considerations as the foregoing that the Doctrine and Covenants section on marriage advises that "marriages should be solemnized in a public meeting. . .prepared for that purpose. . .with prayer and thanksgiving" (D. and C. 111:1b, 2a). This is consistent with its dignity and social consequence. "It is the highest form of social life known to man. . .the most sensitive organism in society" (Elmer G. Homrighausen). Such marriages recognize also that God is a partner in the marital enterprise.

Governments are instituted of God (D. and C. 121:1). Without ordered government there is chaos. Although no government is perfect, improvement is sought by revolution (advancement in harmony with central principles) rather than by rebellion (revolt without regard for central principles). To this end we as citizens seek to distinguish the essential functions of government and support those in authority who exercise these functions. This is part of carrying our share of the governmental burden. Governments, on their part, refrain from interference with the religious beliefs of citizens except as the practice of these beliefs infringes on the rights of other citizens.

We are expected by our faith to be responsible citizens. We are challenged to give enlightened interaction to and with the governments of nations where we reside. Such interaction applies to every aspect of daily life. It includes the full exercise of our franchise. We are called to participate in activities which tend to break down the barriers between people. These include cultivation of skills and craftsmanship, the sharing and creation of great literature, training for and participation in the business of government, as well as the discovery and support of quality men and women who can be relied on to administer the laws with equity and justice.

Questions and Discussion Topics

1. What is meant by marriage "covenants" as found in Doctrine and Covenants 111:2? What are the positive and negative aspects of a marriage relationship? What are their implications?

175

2. Marriage should be contracted only after sober but pleasant and mature consideration of its duties, disciplines, responsibilities, and rewards. What is the meaning of "mature" in this connection? Suggest some obligations this places on the parties, their parents, the church.

3. What is meant by the statement that "marriages...should be solemnized in a public meeting"? Why is this desirable?

4. What is the church's view of marriage today? If you marry out of the church, what obligations does each spouse have? How can members be supported by the local church if they marry out of the church?

5. Discuss the importance of considering both before and within marriage the divine intention that marriage shall be a life-fulfilling union.

6. Compare the view of Doctrine and Covenants 111:4b with the church's current stand on divorce in *Rules and Resolutions*, No. 1034, paragraph 7. How are the views the same and different?

7. What are the just limits of civil governments in relation to worship? What are the implications of the statement that "the civil magistrate should restrain crime, but never control conscience; to punish guilt, but never suppress the freedom of the soul" (D. and C. 112:4c)?

8. What rights must a government secure to its citizens if it is to continue in peace? What integral rights did the framers of the Magna Carta and American or Australian Constitution regard as important?

9. How is Section 112:12b-d colored by the slavery
   issue of the United States in the 1830s and 1860s?
   What may have been reasons for such a statement
   in 1835 and for its endorsement by the
   Reorganization in 1863?

Exploration 40
THE APPENDIX

PREPARATORY READING: Church History, Volume 1,
pages 226-230; Doctrine and Covenants 108
ADDITIONAL BOOKS NEEDED: Bible

Introduction

The revelation recorded in Section 108 of the
Doctrine and Covenants was given November 3,
1831. This was two days after Section 1 (the Preface)
was received. If printed in its chronological order it
should probably follow Section 69. It was intended to
serve as an appendix to the revelations in the Book of
Commandments; and in deference to this intention it
was printed at the end of the revelations in the 1835
edition of the Doctrine and Covenants. This precedent
has been followed in subsequent editions.

For Consideration

The description of Doctrine and Covenants 108 as
"The Appendix" can be misleading if the student fails
to note its historical setting. Apparently the revelation
was not given in answer to a specific request for an
appendix to the Book of Commandments but after a
number of elders sought from Joseph instruction
concerning the preaching of the gospel, the gathering,
and related matters (Church History, Volume 1, page
226). It is possible that the Appendix will be best
understood when it is considered in its setting among
the other revelations received at the conferences held

at Hiram, Ohio, in November 1831 (D. and C. 1, 67, 68, 69).

A major concern of the church toward the end of 1831 was with the gathering. There were many inducements to think of this in physical terms—as moving to the frontiers of opportunity and freedom. But the essentially spiritual nature of the gathering is here reaffirmed. It is from spiritual wickedness in all nations that the Saints are advised to gather to a center of faith and service under God (D. and C. 108:2c, 4b).

Those who gathered looked forward to life made rich in understanding and righteousness by fellowship with the Saints. Every day was to be a day of rejoicing in the Lord. For that very reason every day was to be a day of preparation for greater days yet to come. The more distant end, bringing to culmination all the times of preparation, was the coming of the "great day of the Lord" (D. and C. 108:1, 3d).

The spiritual nature of the Zionic enterprise was emphasized in admonitions which are as pertinent today as they were when first uttered. Among them note the following:

"Sanctify yourselves."—D. and C. 108:2a.

"Be ye clean that bear the vessels of the Lord."—D. and C. 108:2b.

"Let every one call upon the name of the Lord."—D. and C. 108:2c.

The gathering is to be from among all nations. Also, it must be initiated among the Saints where they are in all nations. No sincere believers wait to begin living in the spirit of the gathering. They gather and are gathered into the fellowship of the disciples, renouncing the life of selfishness and entering into the life of love (D. and C. 108:3, 4, 5b, 11d).

The early elders thought of the Restoration as fulfilling the age-old message of Revelation 14:6-7. This is clearly affirmed in Doctrine and Covenants 108:7. Note the elements of the "Angelic Message."

- The gospel is not new. It is rooted in the eternal.
- The gospel is for the people of every nation, despite their superficial diversities.
- The gospel calls on all persons to live in awe before the unmatched majesty of God.
- The gospel sets forth and vindicates the judgmental God as was never before so fully possible.
- The gospel concerns us in our relationship to God and to our fellow beings. This, and only this, is of ultimate importance.
- The gospel's power is found in the worship of God who wrote his holy and loving purpose into all creation; to know God is to know life eternal.

Understanding of the nature and rewards of godliness—its demands and rewards—is not reserved to the wise and prudent (I Corinthians 1:18-21; Matthew 11:25 R.S.V., 11:27 I.V.; Luke 10:2) but to the clean and loving (D. and C. 108:10; Isaiah 35:8). Love is a universal language which carries its own credentials.

There is no forgiveness for those who know the way of love and ignore persistently the call to live in love. The way of love after the pattern of the Lord Jesus is the way of life and salvation. This is the way of the Restoration.

Questions and Discussion Topics

1. What revelation is known as "The Preface"? When was that revelation received? Why is Doctrine and Covenants 108 called the Appendix? When was the Appendix received? Against what background is it best discussed?

2. The Saints were directed to gather in Missouri. Why? (See D. and C. 28:2c, d; 38:7.) They were also commanded to go out from Babylon. What does this mean? What is the relation between these two aspects of the gathering?

3. One of the recurring notes of the Doctrine and Covenants is on the need for preparation. This is particularly evident in the Appendix (D. and C. 108:2a, 3d, 4c, 5c, 5d, 11a). Comment on the nature of the preparation required of the Saints. It is progressive. To what end does it point?

4. Another recurring emphasis throughout the revelations is on the call to repentance. This is to be a keynote of the preaching of the elders (D. and C. 108:5b, 11b). What is the necessity for repentance in relation to the gathering? Discuss the meaning of Acts 11:18, "repentance unto life."

5. The gospel is to be preached in all nations (D. and C. 108:3a, 5, 7). What significance will the doctrine of the gathering have for those whose circumstances make it impossible for them to gather at any time? In this connection note the importance of the Saints enriching their fellowship wherever they are located.

6. The "Angel Message" was prominent in the preaching of the early church and the early

Reorganization. The "Angel Message" tracts were among the most appealing and widely used of those published in this century. Review Doctrine and Covenants 108:7. What elements of this message are timely? How can they be presented today?

7. In what terms is the gospel to be preached (D. and C. 108:11a)? Why is this imperative?

8. The early apostles expressed concern that the Saints should "grow in grace and the knowledge of our Lord and Savior Jesus Christ." These were the last written words of the author of II Peter 3:18 to the early Christians. The apostle Paul considered this a joint achievement (Ephesians 2:19-22; 4:14-16). In what ways are the quality of the caring church fellowship and evangelism related aspects?

THE PERIOD OF 1861-1976

Exploration 41
REORGANIZATION

PREPARATORY READING: *New Commentary*,
399-419; Doctrine and Covenants 114, 115, 116,
117

ADDITIONAL BOOKS NEEDED: Church History,
Volumes 2 and 3

Introduction

The first twenty years of the Reorganization—1853
to 1873—marked a period of struggle for identity.
Those who joined the Reorganization were few in
number, lacked money and experienced leadership,
and had to extend the work in such time as they
could spare from their daily concerns.

The excellent wisdom and high degree of inspiration
of President Joseph Smith III are shown in the church's
course followed during these difficult years. He had
learned well the lessons of Nauvoo and was
determined that the growth of the church should be
sound and well balanced. Key personnel, in addition
to Joseph, were William Marks, Jason W. Briggs, and
Israel L. Rogers.

For Consideration

Such early leaders of the Reorganization as Jason W. Briggs, Zenas H. Gurley, Sr., and William Marks were men of good character. They were convinced of the divinity of the Restoration movement and of their own responsibility in relation thereto. They do not appear to have aspired to leadership but followed other leaders until their own hopes were shattered. When they accepted leadership among those who became charter members of the Reorganization, they did so in response to divine guidance received by them and by other members of the group. Acceptance of his call by Joseph Smith III fulfilled many prophecies and confirmed the faith of those who had prayed for his coming.

Note the background of Doctrine and Covenants 114: the prior discussions, the burden laid on a young prophet, and the nature of this initial prophetic experience (*New Commentary*, page 403).

Note also the principle embodied in the selection of the Twelve to work with the Bishop since Joseph "had not yet approved himself unto the scattered flock" (D. and C. 112:5b; *New Commentary*, pages 404, 438-439).

Strength accrued to the Presidency by virtue of the ordination of William Marks. He brought wisdom, courage, and familiarity with the work of the church under Joseph Smith, Jr. An additional advantage in his ordination was in having two members in the Presidency (Church History, Volume 3, pages 721-726).

It is well to note the attitude of President Joseph

Smith III when differences of interpretation tended to divide the Presidency and Twelve (*New Commentary*, page 408) and the manner in which his example reinforced his counsel (D. and C. 117:13, 122:17, 129:9).

Following the American Civil War and the beginning of the period of Reconstruction many factors had a bearing on the ordination of Negro ministers. Yet today the Reorganization ordains persons of all races to the priesthood. We have grown in our understanding of how we can effectively minister in various cultures. Many changes have occurred in the world which encourage such ordinations. We are called to ordain ministers of every race to leadership among their own people (D. and C. 116:4).

The standing of Joseph Smith III in the church matured from 1860 to 1873. After the membership of the presiding quorums was reconstituted in harmony with the revelation of 1873, these quorums also gained strength. Growth in the strength of the church at this later date is indicated as compared with 1860.

Questions and Discussion Topics

1. What factors led Saints who were dissatisfied with the leadership and teachings of the post-1844 divisions of the early church to reorganize at Beloit and Zarahemla, Wisconsin? What procedure was followed? Who were their leaders? (See Church History, Volume 2, pages 196-198, 200-255; *New Commentary*, pages 399-401.)
2. How did Joseph Smith III regard his acceptance of

his call to be Prophet, Seer, and Revelator to the church? (See Church History, Volume 3, pages 247-250; *New Commentary*, pages 401-402.)

3. What reasons led to the association of the Twelve and the Bishop in 1861? How long did this close association continue? Why was it discontinued? What does this imply concerning the basic relation of the Presidency and Presiding Bishopric?

4. What important missionary principle was reemphasized in 1865? To what fields does this apply most particularly (*New Commentary*, page 406)? Explain why it may still be important (D. and C. 135:4).

5. How were the members of the Twelve selected in 1835? in 1853-1873? since 1873? How have the presidents of the Twelve been chosen (*New Commentary*, pages 412-413)?

6. What instruction was given in 1873 concerning stakes (D. and C. 117:11)? How was this altered in 1901 (D. and C. 125:10)? How does the church interpret these revelations today? How many stakes does the church currently have? What are the basic differences between stakes and districts?

7. Why was it necessary to indicate by revelation the acceptability of "the different organizations for good" in the church (D. and C. 118:12)? What kinds of organizations were they? Discuss, briefly, the result of this approval.

8. For what reasons might we regard the revelation of 1873 as marking the end of an era in the history of the Reorganization?

Exploration 42

PRINCIPLES OF STABLE GROWTH

PREPARATORY READING: *New Commentary*, pages
419-429; Church History, Volume 4, pages 404,
475-479, 481, 483-485, 535, 537, 539-545,
561-562; Doctrine and Covenants 118, 119

Introduction

Eight years elapsed between the revelation of 1865
(D. and C. 116) and that of 1873 (D. and C. 117).
Another nine years passed before the revelation of
1882 was received (D. and C. 118) and five more
before the very important revelation of 1887
(D. and C. 119). During this extended period there
were no additions to the personnel of the Presidency
or Twelve, although there were losses due to sickness
and death. There were but seven members of the
Twelve at the opening of the conference of 1887.

This was an important period, nevertheless, in terms
of the growing maturity of the general officers, the
numerical growth of the church, and the progress
toward stability in the church and in major local
centers.

For Consideration

By 1882 it had been almost thirty years since the
initial movements toward the Reorganization. Until
this time a major emphasis had been on the
enlistment of those who had been members of the
church prior to 1844 and their children. This ministry

was to continue (D. and C. 119:4), but in the nature of things it soon gave place to a more general missionary appeal. To this end it was important that the church should be united in faith and endeavor under leadership similarly united.

The situation concerning the mission in Chicago illustrates one of the problems of the period. Almost all of the branches of the time were in rural or semi-rural areas. The urban setting of the Chicago mission called for a different approach, and disagreement arose. The counsel given was twofold: (a) do not spend more time now on what is essentially an administrative problem, and (b) let the appropriate district officers work toward a solution.

At this time there were few districts and the members of the traveling ministries tended to regard them as organizations of convenience which had no substantial authority. The instruction concerning the Chicago mission affirmed the authority of district officers in local situations, but in actual fact, few of the local officers had presiding experience. The traveling ministry (the Twelve and Seventy) were more likely to be acquainted with administrative situations. The instruction now given was soundly pertinent to the needs of the church in this regard. It said, in effect, that local presiding officers (especially at the district level) should be respected in their places but that these local officers should "honor and pay heed to the voice and counsel" available to them from the more experienced ministers.

Problems of local organization were accompanied by differences concerning the faith and practice of the church. Some pushed their opinions so aggressively as to cause division and this some of the Saints resented. One possible procedure was to refuse to sustain those held responsible for division. Again twofold counsel was given: (a) the Saints were to consider with patience the effect of their actions on the good of the work and (b) those pushing their opinion to the detriment of the Cause must remember their primary and inescapable responsibility to God as stewards (D. and C. 118:4).

In the revelation of 1887 four of the elders were called to the Twelve. This gave the quorum eleven members, the number "expedient" at this time. The wisdom of this action became apparent in the years immediately ahead when a unanimous decision by the full Quorum of Twelve might have hampered the administration of the Presidency which had only two members after the release of David H. Smith in 1885.

The time and manner of the administration of the Sacrament had been among the areas of division. The revelation of 1887 pointed out that "contention is unseemly" and applied this principle where it obviously had full justification. It was recognized that some would refrain from partaking of the emblems under the pattern now set forth, but even so the elimination of contention was to be sought (D. and C. 119:5g).

A hundred years ago musical instruments which were used at dances and in similar situations were often considered unsuited to use in worship. The counsel given in this connection was insightful for its day, even though many now take it for granted. In worship the attitude of the worshipers is of central importance, not the means used. Yet decisions as to the use of these means should be made in light of the situations within the fellowship.

Note with what patience the problem of Sabbath observance is addressed. The primary concern in the instruction here given, as evident throughout the revelation, is to eliminate contention while observing essentials.

Questions and Discussion Topics

1. Why was it not expedient to open new missions abroad in 1882? For what reasons was it also not expedient to fill the presiding quorums?
2. What instruction was given regarding counsel of the traveling ministry? Why was this instruction especially necessary at that time? What conditions were to be met by the traveling ministry? How may this counsel be considered wise today?
3. Review and discuss the importance of the instruction given concerning the mission in Chicago. How have the principles involved been settled with the growth of the church and the acceptance of regular procedures? What is the relationship of branches to districts today?
4. Under what conditions was the revelation of 1887 received? What changes took place in the Quorum of Twelve in harmony with this revelation? For what probable reason was the quorum left unfilled?
5. How is the instruction given "the elders and men of the church" in Doctrine and Covenants 119:2-3,

9 appropriate today?

6. Review and list the instruction given concerning the Sacrament and music in worship. What are the principles involved? How are their applications the same for us? Different?

7. What is the instruction of 119:7 in regard to the Sabbath? In what way was this tentative? What principle concerning a person's worth is noted?

8. In what ways are the revelations of 1882 and 1887 important in the life of the church today?

Exploration 43

TRAVELING AND STANDING MINISTRIES

PREPARATORY READING: *New Commentary*, **pages 429-442; Church History, Volume 4, pages 641, 644-645, 653; Volume 5, pages 92-96, 143-144, 147, 207-208, 241-243, 245-247, 250-263**

Introduction

The trend toward further clarification of the functions of local administrative officers continued. In general the Twelve and Seventy recognized the need for this clarification, but they felt that adjustments should proceed under their direction. The epistle of the Twelve (1887) as revised (1888) set forth the position of the Twelve and Seventy but was not acceptable to the First Presidency nor to many of the high priests. (See historical note introducing Section 120.) In 1890 the Twelve asked for divine direction, promising to sustain President Smith as he sought the needed light. Four years later still further clarification was felt to be needed and a similar procedure was followed.

For Consideration

In our attempt to understand the revelations of this period it is important that we keep in mind such factors as the organizations, persons, and quorum traditions which were involved (Church History, Volume 5, page 92); the widely held sense of the priority of missionary work (Church History, Volume 4, page 480); and the feeling of the Twelve and Seventy that since many branches needed membership to give them stability the traveling ministry, at their convenience, must be free to minister in these branches.

The revelation of 1890 was addressed to the Presidency and Twelve who had asked for light and were primarily concerned with what was now stated. It was, of course, available to all who were interested. The revelation of 1894 was addressed to the elders. Its content was thus recognized as a concern of the entire Melchisedec priesthood and no longer remained a matter for determination in discussion between the Presidency and Twelve.

Branches, congregations, districts, and stakes do not bring themselves into being. They are organized on the authority of those of the administrative offices and conferences having jurisdiction. The reason for this is twofold. (1) the work of the church in adjacent areas must be considered in relation to various types of organization. (2) In effecting such organization the responsible officers affirm that the local Saints are now of sufficient numbers and experience to manage their own affairs under the direction of the available members of the standing ministry.

The Twelve and Seventy are "traveling ministers and preachers of the gospel to *persuade* men to obey the truth" (D. and C. 120:3b). The traveling here envisioned is that which is involved in pushing their ministry into other fields (D. and C. 122:7a, c). It is such traveling as leads to new openings. It may be to distant lands or it may be to some nearby area where the planting of the work at this time is especially pertinent.

The work of the standing ministry as here set forth has to do with the basic character of the Saints. It has notes of permanence and social witness. It makes clear that the work of the pastoral arm of the church is as important as that of the missionaries.

It took several years for the Presidents of Seventy to find their place in the church structure and provide for continuity in office of the Seventy. This was remedied to some degree at the conference of 1885 (D. and C. 121:5b). Seventies had been recommended for ordination prior to this time by the apostles in the several fields. The instruction given in 1890 (D. and C. 120:10) brought the current practice in closer harmony with the law and relieved the Twelve of responsibility which they had carried because of the prior lack of Presidents of Seventy (D. and C. 104:43; 120:10).

Note the clear and forthright statement of the calling and responsibilities of the president of the church and his counselors with which the revelation of 1894 opens. The importance of agreement concerning the law and doctrine of the church had been set forth long before (D. and C. 41, 42), but the agreement desired was not to be achieved by a mere sharing of opinions. To be effective it must be according to the spirit of wisdom and understanding and the light of revelation.

The two most pressing concerns of the church in 1861 had been in the areas of missions and finances.

His ordination as president of the high priesthood and of the church gave Joseph Smith III major responsibility here, as in every field of church endeavor; but in the existing situation the Twelve were called to carry some of the burden (D. and C. 122:5). That the burden could be transferred back to the Presidency in 1894 was made possible by Joseph's acceptance by the Saints and was in harmony with the general tenor of this revelation. The Twelve were to continue specified general responsibilities in connection with temporalities but were freed of detailed administrative concern.

Questions and Discussion Topics

1. State the situation in which the revelation of 1890 was given. To whom was it addressed? What was the significance of this address? In what spirit was the revelation received?
2. Who may preside over a branch? What priorities of office would be considered in this connection? Who may and may not preside over a district?
3. What is the difference between the "traveling ministry" and the "standing ministry"? What members of the priesthood are in each group? What offices belong to either group in suitable circumstances?
4. Who are the "traveling presiding councils of the church"? What ministers are especially authorized to take cognizance of matters which involve the law and usages of the church and its general interests? Should general officers adjust local difficulties of long standing or should they require

local authorities to do so?

5. Through whom are elders called to the office of Seventy? From what quorums are seventies usually selected? What is the specific work of the Seventy?

6. Did the revelation of 1890 settle the issues then confronting the Presidency and Twelve? Why? If more counsel was needed, what more was needed? How is this problem characteristic of parallel situations?

7. Upon whom rests the burden of the care of the entire work of the church? Which quorum is "next in authority in spiritual things"? Why is definition of official prerogatives important? Is a precise verbal definition usually satisfactory? Why? Why not? What quorums take precedence in unorganized territory? Which ministers are second in authority in missionary situations? Who presides over the local work of the church?

8. What change was made in the relation of the Twelve and the Presiding Bishopric in accordance with the revelation of 1894? On whom was placed the responsibility which hitherto had been carried by the Twelve? What principle was involved in the temporary assignment of responsibility to the "quorum next in authority" after the Presidency?

Exploration 44

A MATURING ORGANIZATION

PREPARATORY READING: *New Commentary,* pages 443-460; Church History, Volume 5, pages 213, 220, 313-314, 388-389, 391-399, 423-424, 616-641; Doctrine and Covenants 124, 125, 126

Introduction

Our concern in this study has been with the Book of Doctrine and Covenants. This has required us to give attention to the background of the revelations in the history of the church. But advances not mentioned in the revelations were taking place. The Daughters of Zion, the Sunday School, and the Religio, made significant contributions in the 1890s. In that decade both Graceland and the Saints Home were launched. The Saints were beginning to push toward institutional maturity.

For Consideration

The death of W. W. Blair in 1896 left President Smith without counselors. The choice of Alexander H. Smith and E. L. Kelley to serve as counselors for a limited period brought to his side one who had been president of the chief missionary quorum of the church and also the chief financial officer of the church. This emphasized the moral authority of members of the Presidency to carry among them "the burden of the care of the church" (D. and C. 122:2).

The designation of Alexander H. Smith to be

197

Presiding Patriarch reminded the Saints that Joseph Smith, Jr., and his brother, Hyrum, had been associated in such a ministerial relationship as would now exist between Joseph Smith III and Alexander. Alexander Smith continued to serve as Presiding Evangelist after he had been released from the Presidency and his relation to the president of the church continued to be close. In this connection note the introduction to Appendix A (D. and C. 107) in the 1970 edition of the Doctrine and Covenants and also the content of paragraph 29b-f.

With the other general quorums filled, it was now natural to look toward the strengthening of the Seventy. Instruction received concerning the organization and quorum functioning of the Seventy gave the Council of Presidents of Seventy and the body of Seventy a measure of self-perpetuation which is unique in church organization (D. and C. 124:5-6). Since the Presidency and Twelve are the appointing authorities of the church, however, it has been found wise to consult with them concerning the selection of the Presidents of Seventy and the Seventy. The Presidency and Twelve make every endeavor to be available for such consultation and at the same time to leave both initiative and decision concerning the Seventy with their presidents.

The duties of the patriarch-evangelists now set forth place these officers among the standing ministry. They are freed from administrative responsibilities so as to center their attention on the nurture and revival of the Saints. The giving of patriarchal blessings is one aspect of this total ministry.

The structure of World Conferences is of great importance. It is here that the general officers of the church are chosen and sustained. World Church policies and supporting appropriations are discussed and determined. It is necessary that the conference membership shall be large enough to give adequate representation to the body of the Saints, but it is also necessary that the conference shall be small enough to function effectively. To increase the number of conference members does not necessarily protect and promote democratic ends. Delegates should be well informed and of sound judgment. They meet to discuss and enact. For the legislative agreement to be richly fruitful it must be more than casual concurrence. In the nature of the situation adjustments in the makeup of World Conferences will be made from time to time. In all probability as the church grows there will continue to be the emergence of regional and national conferences. These will function along lines recommended by general authorities and set by the World Conferences. This development will leave to regional/national conferences matters of local importance.

Some members' feelings that they were directed by the Holy Spirit have led them to give direction which was a rightful concern of church officers: voicing calls to the priesthood, commanding or disapproving procedures, admonishing or rebuking the Saints. At times this has become a source of confusion. Action according to the principle set forth in Doctrine and Covenants 125:14 is vital to sound church government.

The world mission of the church was illustrated and promoted by the call to the apostleship of Peter Andersen of Denmark in 1901 and John W. Rushton of England and C. A. Butterworth of Australia in 1902, and by the ordination of local bishops in England (Thomas Taylor), Australia (George Lewis), and Polynesia (Metuaore). It was affirmed, moreover, by the instruction to provide foreign language tracts and by the initiation that new missions might be open at the discretion of the Twelve.

The transfer of some of the older members of the Twelve to the order of evangelists was significant. No promotion or demotion was intended. It appears to have been a more advantageous use of ministerial personnel. Work in the Order of Evangelists gained recognition; it was seen that patriarchal ministry is of such importance as to command the services of men of apostolic caliber.

In harmony with the instruction concerning the Bishopric and the temporal law (126:10) and pursuant to a recommendation of the World Conference of 1910, the Bishopric published a booklet titled *The Law of Christ and Its Fulfillment*. Prior to this time President Smith had written of this matter (*New Commentary*, pages 457-458). It should be noted that his comments were in harmony with the instruction in Doctrine and Covenants 125:14c and that instruction has application in many areas (D. and C. 122:1).

Questions and Discussion Topics

1. Who was involved in the interim calls to the Presidency in 1897, in the changes in the

200

Presidency in 1902, and in the Twelve in 1901 and 1902? What implications may we draw from these calls?

2. What are the duties of Presidents of Seventy? How are the members of this council currently selected? By whom are the Seventy selected? What consultation is involved in approving these selections? Who has the final authority for the ordination of the Seventy? What, if any, presiding functions apart from the Quorums of Seventy do the Presidents of Seventy have?

3. What are the distinctive duties of evangelists? Through whom are evangelists called? Have there been any exceptions to this procedure (D. and C. 126:13)? What later instruction has been given concerning the work of evangelists (D. and C. 137:4b-c)?

4. What are the functions of World Conferences? What is the reason for including ex officio members in the personnel of World Conferences? What ministers have ex officio standing in World Conferences? What are duties of delegates to World Conferences? Why is it desirable that the number of members at World Conferences shall be kept within workable limits? How may changes in conference membership be compensated elsewhere?

5. What notable advance in local organization was made in 1901? Who are the official personnel of a fully organized stake? How are stakes brought into being?

6. What significant changes having to do with world missions took place in the personnel of the

presiding quorums during this period? When were the first bishops ordained in our world missions?

7. What was the instruction given concerning spiritual gifts, local administration, and prophecy in relation to administration to the sick?

8. Contrast the modes of revelation in connection with Doctrine and Covenants 124 *(New Commentry*, page 444), 125 *(New Commentary*, page 446), and 126 *(New Commentary*, pages 455-6).

Exploration 45

INSTITUTIONS AND FINANCES

PREPARATORY READING: *New Commentary*, **pages 460-471; Doctrine and Covenants 127, 128, 129**

Introduction

At the conference of 1906 President Smith was in his seventy-fourth year. It is evident from the inspired documents which he brought to the church in the remaining years of his life, including "The Letter of Instruction," that he was concerned with the functions and personnel of the presiding quorums and with the implementation of the doctrine of the gathering.

For Consideration

Guidance concerning the Sanitarium was given Joseph Smith III before the revelation was received. Note the purpose of the Sanitarium and the relation of the medical, social, and spiritual ministries contemplated in that building.

There was a place for the laying on of hands in the ministry of healing. The consistency of Elder Luff's ministry as church physician and as a spiritual leader was noted.

The recognition of the work of the Daughters of Zion led to the establishment of the children's home as a partial fulfillment of the instruction given in 1873 (D. and C. 117:12). For the principle involved see Doctrine and Covenants 58:6c-f.

The principle prompting the building of the Sanitarium is that healing is connected with the whole person. Ministry to the physically ill may well call on such spiritual resources as faith, hope, patience, and courage. Ministering to the dying or those permanently injured as well as their families may draw even more directly on spiritual resources.

Joseph Smith III was concerned that the church should avoid the pitfalls of debt. Today our society's economic system has changed. The use of credit is an important aspect of modern financing, but the sound use of indebtedness principles is of vital importance. This the church and society learned in the 1930s. Moreover, the instructions noted in Doctrine and Covenants 125:16a and 127:4a are not negative. They call for care and wisdom. The rate at which the church moves forward while avoiding debt is strongly influenced by the teaching and observance of the financial law.

The ministry of comfort and encouragement here recognized as an important obligation of the church toward the Saints in the South Sea Islands is a permanent element in the life of the church (D. and C. 127:5). It unites the Saints in a worldwide fellowship of mutual helpfulness (D. and C. 153:9).

In Sections 127:7 and 128 note the importance of the instruction concerning the gathering. Counsel is provided regarding the function of the Bishopric in relation to stewardship and the gathering. Joseph Smith, Jr., further clarified the role of the general authorities in connection with the Bishopric regarding the promoting and implementing of the gathering.

Elders Joseph Luff and Heman C. Smith were released from the Twelve while they were yet comparatively young. This did not relieve them of ministerial responsibility. Others had been released because of age and the burden of the apostolic calling, but this was the first example of the release of senior ministers in order for them to give their time and strength in specific areas. It suggests the importance of the work in the areas in which each ministered (D. and C. 129:2, 3).

Questions and Discussion Topics

1. What was the background of the revelation of 1906? What does this indicate about the functioning of the prophetic office in preparation for revelation? What were the major points of concern at this time?
2. What is the relation of healing to the concept of wholeness? In what ways is the ministry of the church involved in health ministries? What were the instructions regarding facilities for this ministry? How does Section 127:2 call for a joining of the skills of physicians and ministers?
3. Recapitulate the instruction concerning the gathering which was renewed in these revelations. What was added concerning selfishness and speculation? Of what importance are these instructions to our lives today?
4. When was President Frederick M. Smith called to the First Presidency? When was he called to be president of the church? By what important

document was the procedure in this matter governed?

5. Why is it important that the gathering be in full harmony with existing civil law?

6. Who is to direct the physical aspects of the gathering? What area is referred to in the term "regions round about"? How is the principle of gathering applied in areas away from the Center Place? How is this application consistent with instructions given?

7. What types of stewardships (organizations) appear to be contemplated in this revelation? What is the relationship between stewardship groups and surrounding persons or citizen groups? What are the strengths of such stewardship organizations? Weaknesses?

8. Who are in charge of the temporal affairs of the church? Do they operate independently? What instruction was given in the revelations under consideration regarding those with whom the bishops should take counsel? Note Sections 149 and 149A in this connection.

Exploration 46

THE END OF AN ERA

PREPARATORY READING: *New Commentary*, pages 472-477; Church History, Volume 6, pages 373, 433-435, 469, 485-490, 533-537, 557-577; Doctrine and Covenants 130, 131

Introduction

During the closing years of his life, and especially after the conference of 1909, President Joseph Smith III showed deep concern for the development of mutual understanding and the spirit of cooperation which should ease the transition from his administration to that of his successor. This concern is reflected in his important "Letter of Instruction" and in the paragraphs dealing with lineal priesthood in the revelations of 1913 and 1914.

For Consideration

Joseph Smith III was fully aware that his own lineage was a factor in his call to lead the church. He knew, also, "the tradition of the elders" concerning lineage and the office of Presiding Patriarch (D. and C. 107:29) and other evangelists (D. and C. 104:17, 28), the Presiding Bishop (D. and C. 68:2; 83:3; 104:32a, 34a), and the high priesthood in general. In considering the leadership needs of the church prior to the conference of 1913 President Smith appears to have taken lineage into account. However, lineage is not the only principle involved

(D. and C. 127:8c).

The revelation of 1913 does not mention their lineage in connection with the calls of Apostles Aylor and Hanson. This does not mean that it was unimportant, for their lineage may have been "hid from the world with Christ in God" (D. and C. 84:3). The only requirement laid on them was faithfulness in their apostolic duties. Both this obligation and the promise of needed blessings were given equally to all who were called.

The principle of lineal priesthood illustrates and confirms the concern of our divine Father for the welfare of people down the generations. Some people find it difficult to accept this concept because of confusion over the nature of human freedom. But our freedom is freedom under the God who made us and who set us in our places to serve him and his people. The service which we give is strengthened by understandings, skills, and love which are demonstrated by parents. Thus we are empowered by generations before us.

After mentioning the call of the sons of the leading officers of the church, the revelation continues: "There are others still in reserve who are fitted through the testimony that Jesus is the Christ and the doctrine is true to serve as those who are sent as apostles of peace, life, and salvation" (D. and C. 130:9c). This is the keynote. No matter what lineal heritage a priesthood member has, this central qualification is required. Priestly heritage may be deeply hidden, but if a man is qualified at this point his calling is justified.

The new members of the Twelve were "to take with others of the quorum active oversight of the labors in the ministerial field" (D. and C. 130:4a). This reflects a gradual change in emphasis of the work of the Twelve. In early years they were best known for their able personal ministries. Their supervising ministries were comparatively minimal. With the growth of the church and of the missionary force, the apostolic functions of field administration and supervision were in greater demand.

Debt limits freedom. The counsel to discharge indebtedness is also coupled with the avoidance of unnecessary expenditures which hamper fulfillment of the primary purposes of the church. This message is addressed "to the church assembled and at large"—all members as well as the body.

The principle of sacrifice for the work's sake is not merely economic. It is basic to discipleship. It merits consistent observance in both private and public expenditures. This counsel was reiterated in 1964 (D. and C. 147:5b).

Note the importance of the instruction concerning quelling the spirit of distrust, suspicion, and accusation (D. and C. 130:8). One of the factors fostering this spirit among the membership was the concern of some that education would be regarded as more important for ministry than spirituality. Such suspicion was fed by many factors and needed to be brought under control.

Questions and Discussion Topics
1. What factors led to changes in the Quorum of

Twelve in 1913? When elders were released from the apostolic quorum what was the effect of this release in terms of their apostolic witness? What priesthood did they continue to hold?

2. Give examples of the operation of the law of lineage in the selection of church leaders. What other principles operate to determine the call of leaders?

3. Note Old Testament examples of the operation of the law of lineage. In what ways does consideration of the lineal factor in a priesthood call emphasize the age-long concern of balancing divinity and human needs? In what ways do lineage expectations pose problems for personal self-development? How can the membership support individuals in personal selection of vocations and roles?

4. What are the principles laid down in the revelation of 1913 in relation to the retirement of the church debt?

5. Discuss the instruction given concerning "the spirit of distrust and want of confidence." Note the connection between this instruction and D. and C. 125:14c.

6. In what ways were emphases in apostolic ministry required to change because of church growth (D. and C. 141:6a)? With what central principles must such changes be consistent?

7. Discuss the light thrown on the process of revelation by the statement of President Smith that his task was "to take a careful survey of the whole field" and then transmit the word of the Master in

connection therewith (D. and C. 131:1). In what ways was President Smith limited in seeing the full import of the inspired instruction communicated by him (*New Commentary*, pages 475-476)?

8. Not infrequently the spirit of distrust and lack of confidence in those called to serve in responsible positions (D. and C. 130:8; 131:4) has been accompanied by deep personal concern for the cause of the kingdom. What was this situation? How may that still be a problem for us? How can we work to remove distrust?

Exploration 47
CHURCH GOVERNMENT

PREPARATORY READING: *New Commentary,* **pages 478-493, 563-564; Church History, Volume 7, Preface, pages 55-56, 83-84, 115-118, 172-173, 177-178, 195-198, 326-328, 387-389, 592-593, 625-639, 651-656; Volume 8, pages 69-70; Doctrine and Covenants 132, 133, 134, 135**

Introduction

In preparing some aspects of the transition from his administration to that of his successor, President Joseph Smith III made a major contribution. There were administrative problems of long standing, however, on which little progress had been made. Some, like the reorganization of the Presiding Bishopric, were ripe for attention. With regard to these little difficulty arose (D. and C. 132). Others, such as the nature of the field responsibilities and ministries of the Twelve, were approached with considerable uncertainty and soon became causes for disagreement and conflict (D. and C. 133, 134). Superficially it appeared that many of the difficulties arose from personality conflicts. There is an element of truth in this, but the more fundamental problems centered in the nature of the authority of the President of the church and the quorum of the First Presidency, its limits and balances.

For Consideration

It had been anticipated that E. L. Kelley would be

succeeded as Presiding Bishop by Edwin A. Blakeslee, who had been Bishop Kelley's counselor since 1891 and was now in the prime of life (D. and C. 130:5; 131:2). When Bishop Blakeslee preferred·not to serve, the church turned to Benjamin R. McGuire who was an active high priest, nearly thirty-nine years old. McGuire was favorably known in the East but was comparatively unknown to the Saints in general. Elder McGuire was welcomed into the church's leadership on the basis of President Smith's statement that the choice was dictated by the voice of the Spirit to him.

One of the great phrases of the early Reorganization was "the hastening time." President Smith believed with all his heart that the hastening time was "upon us." It was around this concept that he pleaded for greater confidence in those chosen for positions of leadership, more devoted consecration of talents and substance on the part of the Saints in general, and urgent church-wide cooperation in the work of the kingdom (D. and C. 132:3-4; 135:2b-c).

In the introduction to the revelation of 1920 President Smith stated that he had given much thought and prayer to the general missionary needs of the church and the condition of the Quorum of Twelve. He had shared the product of this consideration, and the light he had received, with the Quorum of Twelve prior to the conference of 1919 and reported this to the conference of that year (Church History, Volume 7, page 328). The revelation of 1920, which was approved by vote of 701 to 1, reaffirmed earlier instruction concerning the primary missionary responsibility of the Twelve (D. and C.

104:12; 105:7-8; 120:3). The assignments of the Twelve in 1920 looked toward the wide extension of missionary testimony.

The revelation of 1922 was approved by a divided vote, although its content (except for the changes in official personnel) was but a restatement of what had been said in earlier revelations. The major objection to the approval of this document was the proposed removal from the Twelve of three of the apostles who had been involved in the debate concerning apostolic functions. The fourth apostle released was C. A. Butterworth who was in Australia. It is difficult to see how retaining them in the Twelve until debate was ended and then implementing their release would make any permanent difference in quorum relations. Newcomers could hardly be bound by the decisions made by their predecessors under these circumstances.

The development of a quorum tradition can be of great value to those who, on entering the quorum, become the heirs of the distilled experience of their quorum forebears; but times change. To be of value tradition must register legitimate adjustments to changes. Following the conference of 1873 it was 1902 before as many as five newly ordained apostles again entered the quorum. Time was required to assimilate into the quorum the six apostles ordained in 1922.

At times the phrasing of the revelatory documents of President Frederick M. Smith sounded terse and even authoritarian. Some sharply resented the command to "let contention cease," which was set forth in a single paragraph of the document of 1922.

Yet the revelations through Joseph Smith III contain similar but more smoothly phrased counsel (D. and C. 117:13; 119:5a, g, 6; 122:4a), and Frederick M. Smith had used it twice in the well-received document of 1920 (133:2b, c). When we consider it quietly, and are not involved in an abrasive dispute, we know that "contention *is* unseemly" among the Saints.

The revelation of 1925 was a sequel to extended debate on the principles of church government and the adoption of what was known as "the document on supreme directional control." This instruction was given in response to the request of the conference for divine guidance as to whether members of the Presiding Bishopric should be continued in office. Although Bishop McGuire and his counselors were relieved of further responsibility, they retired with the respect and affection of the church.

The conference of 1926 adopted a mild and conciliatory statement concerning the 1925 action on church government. The spirit in which this further action was taken bears testimony that the basic problem in the 1925 conference was emotional. Sides had been taken before the conference opened. Feelings were deeply involved. Minds appeared to be closed even to God's Spirit. Only time and the recapturing of the spirit of kinship under God could bring secure peace.

Questions and Discussion Topics
1. The majority of those called to serve in positions of official responsibility are known among the Saints, and their abilities and experience commend them.

Discuss the unusual burden borne by President
Smith when he was required to bring before the
church the names of ministers who were
comparatively unknown. This occurred in 1916
and 1922.
2. Comment on the meaning of the phrase "the
hastening time." Note in this connection Doctrine
and Covenants 118:1a and the variants in Doctrine
and Covenants 132:3a, 135:2b, 141:5.
3. What factors were at the root of the difficulties
between the Presidency and Twelve in 1916-25?
Suggest precautions which study of these
difficulties recommends.
4. What were the principles of missionary
administration set forth in the revelations of 1920,
1922, and 1925? What is their significance for
today?
5. In 1837 the survival of the church was threatened
by differences among leading officers (Church
History, Volume 2, pages 102-103). How was the
situation met? What lesson was there for the early
1920s differences?
6. The elders of the early Reorganization gave serious
consideration to "the tradition of the elders"
(D. and C. 130:3b). What should such a tradition
embody? What are its values? its dangers?
Consider the importance of quorum work in
relation to the shaping and transmission of
tradition.
7. What is the bearing of spiritual factors on the
legislative procedures of the church? Note Doctrine
and Covenants 11:4b, 104:11i.

8. What factors in the revelatory experience are
   emphasized in the messages given through
   President Frederick M. Smith? What does the
   prophet himself contribute? How is this interaction
   between God and prophet important? Is it
   reasonable to expect the prophet to speak
   infallibly? What safeguards are applied to inspired
   documents?

Exploration 48

THE DEPRESSION YEARS

PREPARATORY READING: *New Commentary,* **pages 494-500; Church History, Volume 8, pages 172-180, 223-227, 304-305; Doctrine and Covenants 136, 137, 138**

Introduction

The revelations received through President Frederick M. Smith during and after the financial depression were concerned, in large measure, with changes in the personnel in the presiding quorums and with the importance of unity of action in meeting the problems and opportunities of those difficult times. The importance of the instruction concerning the ministry of the evangelists and the achievement of a better common understanding of ministerial responsibilities should not be overlooked.

For Consideration

The financial situation of the church at the beginning of the depression of the 1930s was critical. The church was very fortunate that Bishops Curry and DeLapp, who were in the prime of life, were available and willing to assume the heavy burden which Bishop Carmichael and his counselors had carried. Their task evidently called for sound business judgment. Of parallel importance were the faith, courage, and steadfastness which they also contributed.

What years of debate had been unable to accomplish was brought about almost overnight. Members of the church throughout the world forgot their differences and joined in sacrificial cooperation to pay the church debt. The church of the 1930s was the church of a united people. One of the slogans of the depression years was "keep the people informed." To this information, good and bad, the Saints responded constructively.

The time called for reconsideration of the program of the church in terms of fundamentals. This led to frank and searching studies by the members of the Presidency, Twelve, and Presiding Bishopric (Church History, Volume 8, pages 172-178). It determined the emphasis in conferences and reunions. This was "pleasing to the Lord" (D. and C. 136:3a) and also to the Saints.

The worldwide character of the church was illustrated in the call to the apostleship of men born and baptized in distant missions. At the close of the conference of 1938 they numbered almost half of the Twelve. Apostles Rushton, Edwards, and Oakman were from England, Apostles Lewis and Mesley were from Australia. Apostle Gleazer, born in Ireland, was baptized in the United States.

The necessary emphasis on the work of the Bishopric called for balanced emphasis elsewhere. The call of the greatly loved Elbert A. Smith to be Presiding Patriarch and the emphasis on the importance of the work of local evangelists stimulated the consistent growth of the Order of Evangelists which has continued since that time. Patriarch-evangelists are now recognized as an important part of the local ministerial structure (D. and C. 122:8e; 125:6a; 129:7a-b).

Elders W. W. Blair and David H. Smith were named in that order when called to be counselors in the First Presidency (D. and C. 117:3). When David was released in 1885 he was referred to as the "second counselor to the President" (D. and C. 121:1a). In the revelation of 1940, Elder Floyd M. McDowell was referred to as "second counselor" (D. and C. 138:1a) despite the fact that since the preceding conference he had been the only counselor in the First Presidency. The idea of priority between counselors in the First Presidency possibly lay behind the statement in the introduction to the revelation of 1946 that the counselors of President Israel A. Smith, J. F. Garver and F. Henry Edwards, were presented to him "in the order named." There has never been any difficulty between the counselors in the Presidency in this regard. Under the law they are equal in holding the keys of the kingdom (D. and C. 87:3a).

Elder L. F. P. Curry served as Presiding Bishop and also as counselor in the First Presidency between October 1938 and April 1940. Bishop E. L. Kelley had served in these dual capacities between 1897 and 1902 (D. and C. 124:2b-c). Both of these were temporary situations and continued only during the emergencies (D. and C. 126:5b).

The final paragraph of the revelation of 1940 provides a fitting conclusion to President Frederick M. Smith's prophetic emphasis and his constant concern with unity in the building of the kingdom.

Questions and Discussion Topics

1. What was the historical background for the revelation of 1932? Name the members of the Presiding Bishopric at the close of the conferences of 1930 and 1932. Who became the third member of the Presiding Bishopric?

2. What is the importance of developing competence as an aspect of spiritual maturity? How is it both a prelude to and a part of effective service?

3. What were the foundations of the unity of the church in the 1930s? How are they important for today and tomorrow?

4. Discuss the cooperation of the Saints in the payment of the church debt as an illustration of the operation of the principle of common consent. Cite other illustrations, e.g., the recognition throughout the church of ordinations authorized and performed locally.

5. The church is called to preach the gospel in all the world rather than to extend the American culture to distant lands. In light of this discuss the importance of participation in the general quorums and councils of those experienced in distant fields.

6. Discuss the duties of the evangelists as set forth in Section 125:3-6 and elaborated in Section 137:4. What basic functions are discharged by the evangelists in local situations?

7. It was not advisable for Presiding Patriarch Alexander H. Smith and Presiding Bishops E. L. Kelley and L. F. P. Curry to continue also as members of the First Presidency. Why was there necessity for mutual understanding and close

collaboration between the Presidency and the presidents of the other general quorums? among the quorums themselves? How is this related to the growth of the church and the increasing complexity of church ministries?

8. Discuss the phrase "Zion and her buildings" (D. and C. 138:3c). What buildings and institutions are important in the development in any Zionic community? Why is it necessary to maintain the spirit of Zion in the functioning of Zionic institutions? How can this be accomplished?

Exploration 49

POST-DEPRESSION CONSOLIDATION

PREPARATORY READING: *New Commentary*, **pages 501-513; Doctrine and Covenants 139, 140, 141, 142, 143, 144**

ADDITIONAL BOOKS NEEDED: Bible

Introduction

When Israel A. Smith became president, the church had been cleared of debt, but many ill consequences of the depression remained. Among the most notable of these was the lack of full-time appointeee ministers of extended experience. The continuity of quorum testimony had been greatly depleted, particularly among the Seventy. Rehabilitation of the Quorums of Seventies became one of President Israel A. Smith's major concerns as it was of the other general officers.

For Consideration

The expression "their apostleship is extended in presidency" used in Doctrine and Covenants 139:1 for the first time in the revelations is, nevertheless, fully consistent with earlier revelations (D. and C. 19:1a). The expression was used again in Doctrine and Covenants 145:3; 148:2; 153:4. It bears scrutiny. Among other things it indicates that the witnessing function of the apostle can be exercised in organized as well as in unorganized activities. Although they serve in a broader field, the members of the Presidency as well as those of the Twelve and Seventy are "special witnesses of the name of the Lord."

It is not unlikely that President Israel A. Smith's prophetic contribution will be best remembered in connection with Doctrine and Covenants 140:5c. It should be noted that the work of preparation and the perfection of the Saints do go forward, though slowly. This spiritual maturing under the constant care of our heavenly Father is our best guarantee for developing Zionic relationships.

The Twelve have major responsibility for opening the work in new places. Some of these new places are important in terms of strengthening and consolidating the work of the church round about the center. Here priesthood from adjacent regions, stakes, and districts can be enlisted for service, while appointee seventies push into more distant and less cultivated fields. The counsel here looks toward balanced growth. New openings in the center are more likely to become early supporting units in church endeavor than are those in distant places.

The church has to be renewed in every generation. The homes of the Saints are among the most available and promising center of Christian life and testimony. Consider the importance of parents and other relatives in this connection.

Note how specifically the dual functions of the counselors in the First Presidency are mentioned in recent revelations. They are named as counselors to the president of the church and also as members of the quorum of the First Presidency (D. and C. 129:5; 134:1; 139:1a; 142:1b; 144:1; 145:2, 3; 148:2; 153:2-4). In more recent revelations they have been named, also, as counselors to the church (D. and C. 145:2; 148:2; 153:2-4).

The distinctive ministry of the Seventy is in opening new fields (D. and C. 104:11c, 13a, 41b, 43c; 120:3b; 122:7, 8c, 8d; 125:12). The Seventy are called through the Presidents of Seventy. During the depression the members of this council had been reluctant to recommend ordaining to the office of Seventy those elders who could not be appointed and so were not free to travel. Traveling, however, is incidental to opening new areas of testimony. Some new areas were becoming available that did not require undue traveling. Apparently anticipated in Doctrine and Covenants 143:3 was the ordination of those called to be seventies—self-sustaining and appointed. Special effort on the part of the church was given to free these important ministers to exercise their ministry to its highest potential.

The elders were instructed to "meet often for study" in preparation for the greater endowment of spiritual power which has been promised and which awaits the ministry when they can receive it (D. and C. 142:4). Note earlier references to the study of the ministry (D. and C. 10:10, 85:36). Note also in this connection John 16:12-13.

President Israel A. Smith gave careful thought over an extended period to the procedure to be followed in selecting his successor in the prophetic office. His concerns centered in the law and traditions of the church, the Letter of Instruction (Section 144), the proper recognition of the Twelve and the Presidents of Seventy and of the quorums and the World

Conference. He hoped to avoid the confusion and the loss of dignity which would be likely to follow any premature publication of his document of May 28, 1952. His clear designation of the call of Elder W. Wallace Smith to be the next president and prophet of the church and the procedure by which the call should be consummated were major factors in the smooth transition in presidential responsibility following his death (D. and C. 144).

Questions and Discussion Topics

1. Since 1946 six members of the Council of Twelve have been called to be counselors in the First Presidency. Of five of these, it was said that their apostleship was to be "extended in presidency." When President Edwards (D. and C. 148:1) and Apostles Hield (D. and C. 147:1), Ettinger (D. and C. 151:3b), and Ralston (D. and C. 152:2b) were relieved of their duties, each was told that he must continue his apostolic witness in his high priestly calling. What light does the foregoing throw on the nature of the apostolic task? (Note D. and C. 83:10b, given September 1832. The Quorum of Twelve was organized in February 1835.)

2. Analyze the meaning of the divine affirmation that "Zionic conditions are no further away, nor any closer, than the spiritual condition of my people justifies." How is this always true?

3. Why is it important that the work of the church near the center shall be consolidated? What is the role of evangelism in the Center Place and regions

round about in relation to the gathering?
4. What is the meaning of the terms "patriarch" and "evangelist"? How are they related? Does the term "patriarch-evangelist" indicate this interrelationship? Why?
5. What is the meaning of the expression "the traveling ministry" (D. and C. 104:13, 41b, 43c; 120:3b)? Is traveling the important phase of their ministry or is their availability to travel when called on or directed by the Holy Spirit of fundamental importance? Why do they travel? What conditions in today's society cause us to view this term differently?
6. Why were the elders advised to "meet often for study"? What is the relation between the study of the scripture and revelation? between study and endowment?
7. What is the function of the quorums and councils of the church in relation to the approval of revelation? Why are inspired documents submitted to organized quorums and mass meetings of the priesthood individually?
8. Indicate the permanent elements (as contrasted with those dealing with personnel) in the revelations given through President Israel A. Smith. On what issues do they focus?

Exploration 50

PERSONNEL AND PRINCIPLES

PREPARATORY READING: *New Commentary*, **pages 513-525; Doctrine and Covenants 145, 146, 147**

ADDITIONAL BOOKS NEEDED: Bible

Introduction

The emphasis in the early revelations of President W. Wallace Smith was on leadership (personnel, authority, support), the callings within the orders of the priesthood, the nature of stewardship, the principles of church government, and the functioning of General Conference. Changes in personnel are necessarily of relatively temporary importance. The instruction concerning stewardship principles and the General Conference are of more permanent significance.

For Consideration

It would be difficult to make a more succinct and yet more comprehensive statement on the situation of a disciple who has died than that which opens the first of the revelatory documents presented by President W. Wallace Smith. It is to be presumed that no explanations based on our earthly experience can convey to us, truly and richly, the realities of the hereafter. What really matters is that the righteous dead are in the care of our wise and loving heavenly Father. "Blessed are the dead which die in the Lord from henceforth" (Revelation 14:13).

The distinctive ministries within the patriarchal order as affirmed in this revelation are to be expected in view of the basic principle that "all are called according to the gifts of God unto them" (D. and C. 17:12a; 119:8b; 46:5a). Individual ministries are exercised within a larger calling shared by others.

Doctrine and Covenants 145:9 indicates that some who are not yet named "are called' to the apostleship. The tense is present, not future. The thought appears to be that some were then serving in places to which they had been properly called and ordained, yet it was the divine intention that they should serve as apostles after further faithful preparation to which their current service would contribute.

Note the reference to the principle of common consent in Doctrine and Covenants 146:2. Having consented to the ordination of leading officers of the church, the Saints are under obligation to receive affirmatively the ministry of these leaders (note D. and C. 125:14c).

The instruction to "let any remaining contentions over minutiae cease" (D. and C. 146:3) is not an attempt to halt serious concern with matters of importance on which unanimity has not yet been achieved (D. and C. 129:9). It is "contention over minutiae," not honest differences of opinion, which is decried. Contention among disciples of the Lord is "unseemly" since it is unchristian. This is basic (D. and C. 117:13). Contention hinders the effective prosecution of the work of the kingdom (D. and C. 98:3; 119:5; 135:2; 136:3).

Note how widely the definition of stewardship in

Section 147:5a broadens the usual stewardship concept. The rich ministry of the Lord Jesus calls for our wisest and most devoted response in every part of our lives and throughout our lives.

The work of the Twelve changes with changing circumstances, but the basic calling of the apostles does not change (D. and C. 147:7). Changes in modes of operation should be merely adjustments to new opportunities to do what is fundamental. Changes in procedure need not be regarded as heretical. Rather, they are ways God works through our best understandings of the day.

Questions and Discussion Topics

1. What is the heart of apostolic witness (Acts 1:8, 22; D. and C. 104:11c)? In what ways do the revelations indicate that apostolic witness may be extended (D. and C. 139:1; 147:1; 148:1, 2)? Is apostolic witness exercised only by members of the Twelve (D. and C. 26:3a; 104:11e; 117:8; 147:2, 3)?
2. What is the importance of diverse ministries within related callings (D. and C. 97:3)?
3. The call of God is written into the structure of the being of those called (D. and C. 119:8b). It is matured under the guidance of the Spirit of God. How can a call be nullified by the failure of those called to respond (D. and C. 127:8)? What is meant by "few are chosen" (D. and C. 92:1d; Matthew 20:1; 22:14)? How is this connected with the obligation of service resting on members of the priesthood and on all disciples?

4. What is the relation of common consent to the support of local and general leaders?
5. What are the functions of church leaders in relation to General Conferences? When was the word "General" changed to "World" in relation to Conference? Why? In what areas of church government does the World Conference operate? In what ways may World Conference guide, limit, or promote World Church administration?
6. What factors tend to change frank discussion over differences into "contentions over minutiae"?
7. The stewardship of temporalities is the special responsibility of the Bishopric. Who else should teach the principles and the practice of stewardship? Why?
8. What is the relative importance of stewardship principles? Identify them. What methods are used in their application?

Exploration 51
EXPANDING AND UNIFYING MINISTERIAL DUTIES—THE TEMPLE

PREPARATORY READING: *New Commentary*, **pages 526-537; Doctrine and Covenants 148, 149**

Introduction

The conference of 1966 saw the church facing foward in a way which had been almost impossible a few years earlier. The sharp divisions of the 1920s were long past. The years of the depression had been weathered with dignity and in unity born of shared sacrifices. New and younger leaders were called into the presiding quorums. Able ministers were being appointed and others were taking up responsible positions of local leadership. It was timely and tremendously heartening that the vision of the world outreach of the church under the leadership of the Presidency and the Twelve could be renewed and approved in unity (D. and C. 148:10).

For Consideration

The increase in the number of capable high priests who could direct and coordinate the work of the standing ministry made it evident that it was no longer necessary for the Twelve or Seventy to be "unduly concerned" with the details of local church administration. More money was available than ever before. People in the political and business realms were beginning to think in terms of one world.

Bishops are high priests who specialize in the ministry of temporalities. The collection and management of temporalities is not an end in itself but a means to further extend the Zionic cause. It is a necessary means. In this sense the work of the bishop is a "necessary appendage" to the work of the high priesthood (D. and C. 83:5; 149:3; 149A). It is important that bishops be recognized and supported in the discharge of their responsibilities (D. and C. 128:2-3; 129:8; 149:3; 149A:1-2).

Of necessity those having responsibilities in temporal affairs must "act in support of leadership given by the spiritual authorities for the achievement of the purposes of the church" (D. and C. 149:3; 149A:1). This does not call for subservience on the part of the bishops, for they should have a consultative part in the formation of procedures involving finances. Where differences persist, appeals can be taken up the administrative line and, if necessary, to conferences that have jurisdiction (D. and C. 149:2).

Members of the Order of Bishops and others found it difficult to accept some paragraphs in the document that later became Section 149. Many felt that what was not set forth would destroy the relative independence of the "men holding the office of bishop under a presiding head acting for the church" in financial matters (D. and C. 129:8b). Members were helped by explanations from President Smith which were embodied in a further inspired document which was joined with Section 149 as 149A. A further point of difficulty was cleared up in the later document. It had been held by some that appeals from local differences over financial matters could be taken to the Presiding Bishopric. Doctrine and Covenants 149A:4 made it clear that appeals go up the administrative line to the First Presidency.

In another connection President Joseph Smith III had said that the Saints cannot withdraw themselves from a "qualified dependence upon their Gentile neighbors" (D. and C. 128:8a). This is in the nature of our life situation and is true in every field. It carries with it great missionary and service possibilities while at the same time it opens the way for many blessings.

A major problem in developing a soundly trained ministry is to secure qualified teachers. This had been of deep concern to some of the leaders of the church for many years. Recently some of the appointee ministers had studied such things as the history of the Christian church, homiletics (ways to improve preaching), and the principles of pastoral ministry in nearby denominational seminaries. They found their studies helpful and their relations with the ministers of these denominations friendly and stimulating. During the interconference period members of the Presidency, Twelve, and Presiding Bishopric exchanged views with these students and some of their teachers. This was undoubtedly part of the background of Doctrine and Covenants 149:4, 5.

The building of the temple for which the church was now instructed to prepare (D. and C. 149:6) will be epoch-marking. No one familiar with the temple expectations of the Saints regards the temple as "just another building." In the revelation now received the temple is conceived as central to the functioning of the church (D. and C. 83:1, 2; 94:3). It is a place of worship, education, and endowment (D. and C. 83:2b; 85:23, 36-44). If those who come to the temple are clean and pure in heart the promise has been given that the glory of the Lord will rest upon it (D. and C. 35:3b, 42:10c, 94:4, 108:1).

When the temple is built in the Center Place its functions will be registered in the materials used in its construction. It will stand as a witness to the faith of the Saints. The prophetic insight which will determine its function will have to be augmented by supporting genius in many fields. It is hardly surprising that determination of these things is reserved to the members of the First Presidency (D. and C. 149:6a).

Questions and Discussion Topics

1. The numerical growth of the church and of local leaders of ability and dedication has made possible some desirable administrative changes which hitherto were not possible. Suggest ways in which the warmth of the intimate fellowship of earlier times can be retained. Is there a point of maximum spiritual vitality for a stake or branch? If so, what factors contribute to it?
2. Into what distinctive functions is the work of the high priesthood divided? What do they have in common?
3. In what sense is the work of the bishop a "necessary appendage" to that of the high

priesthood? What other offices are described as "appendages" (D. and C. 83:5; 104:2, 8)?

4. Certain "orders" are mentioned in the revelation (D. and C. 129:7). Name them. What is the difference between these "orders" and quorums? When a minister leaves one of the orders does he necessarily leave a quorum? May his release cause him to be transferred from a quorum to a more inclusive quorum? Illustrate your answers.

5. Has any group of Saints anywhere in the world ever been able to withdraw from a "qualified dependence on their Gentile neighbors"? What is the meaning of "qualified" in this connection? Name some of the responsibilities and benefits arising from this relationship.

6. What are some of the problems confronting those who teach church members? Can we learn from those not of our faith? What? In what spirit should we seek to learn from others? How does acquaintance with the faith of others help us to bear our own testimony?

7. Why have we not built a temple before now? Will we need further instruction before construction is begun? Why?

8. The building of the temple is to be financed out of surplus. What further factors must be taken into account in making our preparations to build? Will all who participate in temple ministries receive the fullness of possible blessings? Why?

Exploration 52
CHURCH LEADERSHIP

PREPARATORY READING: *New Commentary,* **pages 537-546; Doctrine and Covenants 150, 151, 152**

Introduction

The revelatory documents presented to the church in 1972, 1974, and 1976 were related to changes in leadership personnel and to the problems of the church in the world. The principles underlying the instruction given are of far-reaching importance and call for study in the spirit of prayer.

For Consideration

Many environmentalists regard their activities in these areas as being required by their Christian faith. Among them church members have found additional support for their concern in revelations dealing with these matters (D. and C. 95:3, 6-7; 102:11; 36:10-12; 49:3e; 85:6a-b). They were admonished to give active support to leadership in such fields (D. and C. 150:7). A similar emphasis is made in a later document (D. and C. 151:9).

Both the site of the temple projected for the Center Place and the responsibility for determining its shape and character had already been made known in a revelation addressed to "the Councils, Quorums, and the Church" (see D. and C. 149:6). The instruction given four years later (D. and C. 150:8) appears to be more general. Defining the purpose of the temple and its location within the designated area calls for continual study. This must necessarily be of major concern to the Presidency, Twelve, Presiding Bishopric, and, very possibly, the Standing High Council.

The earlier of the recent references to the temple indicates that "the full and complete use of the temple is yet to be revealed," but two things are noted: there will be no provision for secret ordinances and there will be provision for "instructional opportunities" (D. and C. 149A:6). Teaching the priesthood is again mentioned in the revelation of 1972. Such intimations of the temple purpose will have an important bearing on its size and general structure. Reflection on the fact that Kirtland Temple is too small to accommodate meetings of the Quorum of High Priests suggests the possibility of ancillary buildings in a temple complex.

In view of the hatred of polygamy throughout the Reorganization there was considerable disquietude among the Saints when it was learned that some polygamists had been baptized in world regions where polygamy was legal and of economic importance. In this revelation it is recognized that refusal to baptize any who are in this situation is no final solution to this problem. The approach of ministry to polygamists, as to all, should be conditioned in faith and love. The determination of procedures is left to the Twelve.

The church does not advance on a clearly discerned front line. Pioneers blaze new trails. Sometimes these new trails do not stand the test of time and experience, but in a world which is constantly offering new opportunities and new challenges the hazards of advance are part of the price of progress. The church suffers, as does every similar institution, whenever the pioneers show more concern for methods than they do for principles. And the church suffers, again as does every similar institution, from the restrictive actions of those who feel they must meet today's challenges with yesterday's weapons. The achievement and maintenance of unity is itself a challenge, but it is one which must be met (D. and C. 151:8, 10; 122:13; 129:9; 147:7).

The procedure by which Elder Wallace Bunnell Smith was called to be president of the church was unique in that it provided for him to take office while his father was still alive. In other respects it was akin to that which had happened before. The importance of experience in the Presidency before becoming president of the church was set forth by President Joseph Smith III in 1902 (D. and C. 126:6). President Frederick M. Smith was a member of the Presidency between 1902 and his ordination as president in 1915. President Israel A. Smith served as a counselor in the Presidency between October of 1938 and his call to that office by the revelation of 1940. After this call he served six more years in the Presidency. President W. Wallace Smith was a member of the Presidency from 1950 until he became president of the church in 1958. Although President Wallace Bunnell Smith was not actually a member of the Presidency prior to his ordination as president in 1978, his relation to that quorum was set forth in such a manner as to give him the greatest opportunity for preparation and the greatest freedom possible under the circumstances.

The transition from the administration of President W. Wallace Smith to that of his son was accomplished with unanimity and dignity. It had been fifty-five years since one as young as the incoming president had presided over the destiny of the church. Wallace B. Smith was born July 29, 1929, and at the time of his ordination was less than forty-nine years old. (President Frederick M. became forty-nine in January 1923.) President Wallace B. Smith had been ordained a high priest in 1965 and had served subsequently as a member of the Center Stake Presidency and as a member of the Center Stake Bishopric. For eight years he had been a member of the Standing High Council of the church.

The things which were evidently close to the heart of President W. Wallace Smith throughout his period of leadership were unity in the presiding quorums (D. and C. 145:8; 148:10), enlarged understanding of official duties (D. and C. 145:6; 147:5a; 149:2, 3; 149A:1-4; 150:11b), the elimination of "contention over minutiae" (D. and C. 146:3; 150:12a), the richer understanding and more widespread observance of the principle of stewardship (D. and C. 147:5; 148:9), the support of church leadership (D. and C. 146:2b), the temple (D. and C. 149:6; 149A:5-6; 150:8), and the elevation of the ethical standards of the Saints (D. and C. 150:7; 151:8-10).

Questions and Discussion Topics

1. In what ways are we stewards of the earth in terms of conservation, pollution, waste, the cultivation and enjoyment of the beauties of nature?

2. In what ways can members of the church and the church in general "renounce war and proclaim peace"? How can we avoid extremes on the issues of militarism or pacifism and concentrate on what we can and should do in view of the command of God and the needs of humanity?

3. What is the present duty of the church and of the members of the church in regard to the temple? Name those who have major responsibilities in this connection. Why? What responsibilities do the Saints in general have?

4. How will the temple differ from a well located and well equipped church building? To whom will temple services be available? What activities are likely to center here?

5. We believe polygamy is not approved of God, nor are a multitude of other actions we identify as sins. Disciples of the Lord Jesus are committed to renounce all sin, for "the Lord cannot look upon sin with the least degree of allowance" (D. and C. 1:5f); but recognizing the sinfulness of particular attitudes and practices and acknowledging that they should be renounced and abandoned does not mean that they are thus overcome. Overcoming some of them—anger, unkindness, arrogant pride—may take a lifetime, even generations. At what point in their repentance should sinners (like

us) be permitted to be baptized? Who shall decide?
In what ways can we bear each other's burdens?
How is this part of our theology of forgiveness?

6. The elders of the church had been admonished,
"Let nothing separate you from each other and the
work whereunto you have been called" (D. and C.
122:17b). If the threat of separation from your
brothers and sisters in the faith should confront
you, what question should you ask yourself as you
seek to preserve your unity in fraternity (D. and C.
129:9)?

7. Name the emphasis in the revelations given
through President W. Wallace Smith which you
consider of great current importance. Why?

8. After many difficult years, the church now appears
to be entering a time of great opportunity. Name
some of the most promising factors in our present
situation. Name some of the hazards of our
situation. What elements are basic to our victory
under God?